W9-AZG-450

How to
Negotiate

Successfully in
Real Estate

Tony Hoffman

SIMON AND SCHUSTER
NEW YORK

Copyright ©1984 by Anthony Hoffman
All rights reserved
including the right of reproduction
in whole or in part in any form
Published by Simon and Schuster
A Division of Simon & Schuster, Inc.
Simon & Schuster Building
Rockefeller Center
1230 Avenue of the Americas
New York, New York 10020

SIMON AND SCHUSTER and colophon are registered trademarks of
Simon & Schuster, Inc.
Designed by Irving Perkins Associates
Manufactured in the United States of America
10 9 8 7 6 5 4 3 2 1

Library of Congress Cataloging in Publication Data

Hoffman, Tony.
  How to negotiate successfully in real estate.

  Bibliography: p.
  Includes index
  1. Real estate business. 2. House buying.
3. House selling. 4. Real property—Purchasing.
5. Real property. 6. Negotiation in business. I. Title.
HD1379.H64 1984 333.33'068   84–5440
ISBN 0-671-49775-8

To my wife, Dee, who is my best friend and who went to bed many nights without me so I could meet the deadline.

To Debbie, who changed my Brooklynese into readable English.

To Dan, for the long nights on the word processor rearranging the paragraphs each time I changed them.

To the airlines, who provided hundreds of thousands of smooth flight miles, allowing me to do my writing.

And to the thousands of students who have used my methods and encouraged me to write this book.

Contents

Introduction

In every aspect of our lives we negotiate. We haggle at car lots, arbitrate at the office, confer with our spouses, compromise with our boss, and concede to our children.

In real estate, negotiation plays a vital role. My own introduction to real estate negotiations came many years ago, when I started investing in small properties. I soon learned that buying and selling real estate involved much more than writing offers. To get the best price and terms I had to negotiate for them.

Today, I know very few people whom I would entrust to negotiate a deal for me, but Tony Hoffman is one of them. His approach to negotiating a contract is simple but effective: If you don't ask for what you want, you won't get it.

In this book, Tony outlines a lifetime of negotiating techniques. It is the essence of a career in which success has pivoted on his ability as a negotiator. For you the reader it is as though you are at his side throughout the negotiations, making decisions with him. Sometimes the atmosphere is tense, other times it's easy and casual. Sometimes the reader leaves the negotiating table breathless and excited about the deal just made.

How to Negotiate Successfully in Real Estate will take you into the world of real estate negotiations and show you how to make your deals successful. You will learn how to negotiate as a buyer and then change hats and negotiate as a seller. The techniques are like piano wires, each designed to play a different tone.

How to Negotiate Successfully in Real Estate is the best book on real estate negotiation ever presented and it gives me great pleasure to write this preface because I am well aware of Tony's unique expertise in real estate negotiations. This book belongs in every investor's library; it should be required reading in every business and real estate class. It is an insightful study of human behavior and fascinating to read as well. But even better, it is full of money-making and money-saving ideas that make it invaluable. It could help you save thousands of dollars.

Albert Lowry

Welcome to Negotiation

There are many books written on negotiations, but none that actually show you how to negotiate in a specific area. This book is designed to help you negotiate and make money in real estate, whether you want to buy your first home, become a landlord with a few single-family homes or duplexes, or achieve financial independence by creating your own financial dynasty through real estate.

I believe that reading books and listening to tapes will help you to learn more about new business ventures and to put that knowledge to work for you. I am constantly learning from books and tapes and I have even bought a double-speed tape recorder to increase my intake. Over the last five years I am sure I have listened to hundreds of tapes and read an equal number of books. (My recommendations for them are listed in the back of this book.)

With all the information available about making money in real estate it would seem that everyone presently involved in real estate investment should be very wealthy by now. But very few are. If you can get rich on equity sharing, buying with nothing down, obtaining foreclosures, using paper, growing money trees, or just buying right, why isn't everyone enormously successful? Because it takes more than just the information provided in books and on tapes. You need to know how to negotiate, and negotiation is an art.

To be a good negotiator you must understand that there is more to closing a deal than being right. You have to develop

15

the foresight to see beyond what most people see and to rid yourself of the tunnel vision most of us are taught at a young age. You will have to learn to listen as well as to hear, to learn to see as well as to look.

How well do *you* see? Here's a little test. Take thirty seconds, but no more, to count the number of *F*'s in the following sentence.

> FINISHED FILES ARE THE RE-
> SULT OF YEARS OF SCIENTIF-
> IC STUDY COMBINED WITH THE
> EXPERIENCE OF MANY YEARS.

If you counted three you are part of the 70 percent majority in this country. If you spotted four or five you are among only 20 percent of readers and if you counted six you belong to the elite top 10 percent. If you found seven, however, you need new glasses. There are only six, one in "finished," one in "files," one in "scientific," and one each the three times that "of" is used.

This book will open your eyes to the real world of real estate negotiations. You will be taken step by step through every aspect of a real estate contract. Whether you are a beginner or an expert, a realtor or an investor, you will find ideas and methods that will help you make thousands of dollars and protect you from losing thousands more.

I will share with you the methods that have helped me acquire over $7 million worth of property in five states, without using my own money. You will learn the methods I have taught to thousands of students throughout the country in my one- and two-day seminars, methods that have helped ordinary people like you and me become millionaires!

If you use my suggestions for negotiation in combination with the already proven, sensible everyday ways to acquire real estate, you should achieve your goal of financial independence, and fairly quickly. The hidden fortunes are out there. Here are the keys to unlock the doors to financial independence.

Knowledge + Action + Negotiation = $$$

Recently there has been a rash of books written on the subject of real estate investing and what it can do to build your net worth. Each book suggests a set of invaluable formulas and methods, the little-known secrets that made the author rich and famous.

Once you have read a number of these money-making manuals you find that although the "formulas to success" are unique to each author, the basic concepts are the same:

1. Develop an investment plan.
2. Use other people's money to acquire income property.
3. Improve the value of the building.
4. Move your equity to pyramid your holdings.

The formulas do work. Real estate investing is one of the best vehicles to snowball your dollars into a sizable estate. However, the experts agree that in order to use their "rags to riches" programs you must have imagination, persistence, skill, and a willingness to take whatever actions are necessary to purchase property, increase its worth, and market it.

What This Book Will Do for You

The step-by-step guide to skillful negotiation in this book focuses on the entire scope of real estate negotiation and gives you an in-depth look at what you can do to better your position and create the great deals you may have only read about before. All the examples and cases provide you with information and techniques you can use every day. Study them several times over until you understand the concepts clearly and can practice the methods confidently. Then you will be ready to negotiate skillfully.

The techniques in this book will help you look and act more confident while at the same time improving your concentration and sharpness at the negotiating table. Your objective as a good negotiator is to feel and appear as though your ability to negotiate simply "came naturally." After some practice, your negotiation skills will be as natural as a normal "hello" and handshake.

Each chapter of this book will give you several concrete learning techniques to make your real estate negotiating stronger. The information and ideas will show you how to deal on a daily basis with contractors, buyers, sellers, brokers, lawyers, and tenants. This is a handbook for negotiating and working with people so that you get what you want.

You Need to Develop Your Negotiation Skills

How you *apply* your knowledge, imagination, and skill is what negotiation is all about. How you write your offers, inspect your buildings, or deal with owners and brokers can mean a difference of thousands of dollars to your investment income. How you negotiate your deals will determine the degree of success you will achieve as a real estate investor. Once you have the tools of a shrewd negotiator, you can then use those "formulas of success" to achieve your goals more quickly and with less worry.

Deal Making Is Like Playing Monopoly

Negotiating can be fun. It is just like playing a huge game of Monopoly, except you are dealing with real dollars. Instead of trading "Boardwalk" for "Pennsylvania Avenue," or "Electric Company" for two railroads, you purchase houses or apartments, collect the rents, make improvements, and then exchange them, perhaps for office buildings or shopping centers, until you build your net worth into a sizable estate.

A short while ago, for example, three doctors and I purchased a forty-unit apartment complex in Tucson, Arizona, within forty-eight hours. The doctors live in Milwaukee, and I am in Phoenix. We found a seller who needed to get out, and by following the negotiation techniques I describe in this book, we were able to buy the complex for $600,000, with $75,000 as a down payment, and sell it eighteen months later for $835,000, a 300 percent profit on our investment capital.

In a similar fashion, this same group negotiated the purchase of an office building three years ago in Phoenix, Arizona, for $615,000 with $75,000 down. Recently, we have been offered $990,000 for it. That's an appreciation of 500 percent on our capital in the three years.

The lesson I learned from the "doctor deals" was quite simple: When it comes to investing in real estate, the fantastic deals won't come to you, you will have to go out and get them. If you are willing to get into the market and submit offers and then follow them up with effective negotiation, you will probably do very well. It helps to have done lots of reading ahead of time, but as in Monopoly, you don't get past "GO" by reading the instructions only. You have to get on the board and play.

Negotiation transforms knowledge into dollars. By using just a few of the techniques I apply to every contract or offer to purchase, you too will have the edge it takes to make your good deals great ones. To become a million-dollar negotiator, however, you need to develop a special attitude. One that will enable you to seek out successful situations, not simply follow other people's rules.

In my office I have a sign that reads simply "99%." Most of my clients think that the sign represents the occupancy goal I set for the apartment buildings I own and manage.

However, when a friend complains to me that "the market is down," "interest rates prevent me from buying" or "I'll wait until the market turns around," I point to that "99%" and explain what it really means. You see, 99 percent of the adults in the world are sheep—people who live their lives each day according to the plans of others. They follow the rules their employers set so they may achieve goals that society has outlined for them. Throughout their lives they were taught to follow. As children, teachers "taught" them and society "molded" them into adults, which naturally allowed politicians to "lead" them, bosses to "manage" them, and religious leaders to "guide" them.

It is no wonder that 99 percent of the people on this earth are content to be regulated and manipulated rather than make their own rules and lead their own lives. It is the 1 percent who refuse to be dominated that become the shepherds and in most cases the best negotiators. You don't have to be a sheep. Regardless of your background, you too can be a shepherd.

Believe You Can—and You Will

To be an effective negotiator your attitude is the most important ingredient. If you choose, you can be a good negotiator—but that depends upon you. Each time you approach a deal, remind yourself that you can have anything in life you desire. All it takes is for you to set your goals, start the wheels in motion, create situations, and negotiate.

When I was selling mutual funds in Denver, Colorado, Claude Peay was my first sales manager. Claude is one of the best sales trainers in the world. He taught me more in two years than the average person learns in a lifetime. He taught me how crucial attitude is. If you really believe you can achieve a goal, you will. One time Claude called my wife and had her go out and buy a new car so that I would have to sell more to cover the payments. At another point, he drove me to a shopping center and had me use reverse negotiations to make a sale. He told me to walk into merchants and say, "You don't want to buy a mutual fund, do you?" The "take away" approach actually worked. That afternoon I made two sales. Because I believed in myself I turned a near-impossible situation that normally would not work into the results I wanted.

Thanks to Mal Scheer, another sales trainer, I learned at an early age how to analyze a situation quickly and interpret other people's reactions. Mal has the ability to observe a person once and, just by watching his actions and reactions, know most everything about that person. He can create situations, seize opportunities, and influence others by sizing up the situation and initiating the appropriate action.

Having a leader's attitude like Mal's requires something that most people do not like to do—think. Learning something new is difficult. Most of us are lazy, and have to be pushed to learn new things and use the vast power of our minds. But if you are prepared to put forth a little more effort than you may have in the past, you can become unbelievably successful!

I learned a very valuable lesson shortly before my thirteenth birthday and right before my father's death. Placing two fingers close to the top of his forehead, my father whispered to me, "Everyone is equal from here down. It is this last inch that puts you above the rest." It took me ten years to realize that he was right. I know now you can be extremely successful if you are willing to use your head. With your "last inch," you can do anything you choose, including learning to negotiate.

So, to be a winner in real estate, you must learn to negotiate, and to be a skilled negotiator, you need a leader's attitude. You can decide for yourself what you want and how to go after it. Be a leader! Let the sheep follow you! It is amazing how this attitude will transform your life. By taking control of your life you can create situations that will open doors to opportunities you only dreamed of in the past. With negotiations alone you cannot be very successful. But with skillful negotiation you will have the leading edge, the ability to use that last inch to keep yourself ahead of the sheep.

Doing What Comes Naturally

Sometimes negotiation comes naturally to us. We do not hesitate to exchange the use of the family car for a teenager's completed homework assignment. Most fathers will agree to take the kids to the park as long as they get home in time for the football game. Have you ever shopped at department stores offering sales, specials, and discounts when you would otherwise go elsewhere? At the same time, are you not negotiating with yourself when you choose to save your money for something special rather than spend it today? Each time we select, decide, or make a choice, we do so because we have negotiated with others (or ourselves) as to the value and benefits we will receive.

At the age of six, my daughter is a natural negotiator. Each night approximately halfway through her dinner she complains she is full and cannot eat any more. After a few moments, she asks for dessert. Either my wife or I will insist that she eat ten more bites. Looking at the vegetables she will have to eat, my six-year-old suggests three. We generally settle with about five. A normal routine in many households.

Why then do so many buyers, sellers, and managers of real estate forget to use their "last inch" and fail to negotiate to get what they want? Negotiating skillfully can put dollars in your pocket. It is a technique you can learn. And it is not hard if you have some guidelines.

Some Facts About Real Estate Today

Recently we have seen incredible growth of real estate investing in America. The rate of new construction each year is stable and for now the amount of land we have to build upon is fixed. What is increasing, however, is the number of people who own, or plan to own, homes and other real estate. The effects of the baby boom are being felt. As the twenty-five to thirty-five-year-olds reach the buying age, we see the demand for housing increasing. Today the average American moves every five to seven years, and in his adult lifetime he will sell his house and buy a new one about five times. When we include the real estate investors, the number of sales and exchanges multiplies.

Years ago people bought a house to live in, their piece of the American Dream. Today many people, like yourself, realize the benefits of owning a home as well as a few rental units for investment. So every year more home owners are becoming landlords. Real estate investment programs are mushrooming throughout the nation. Whether the investors are aware of it or not, they are the deal makers. More often than not, their deals make the real estate industry run. How they negotiate, sell, or trade their property may affect your next purchase. Therefore, practical information on how to negotiate will be invaluable to you. The key for you is to know how "they" negotiate. And what "they" do not know, you will learn.

The world of real estate is a dynamic one. How you perform will be determined by your ability to size up situations and negotiate. I want to help you to learn how to handle realtors, sellers, buyers, brokers, title companies, and even attorneys. How to get them on your side and keep them there. Once you discover what the offer/counter-approach involves, you will be able to negotiate skillfully as a buyer or seller. But it is up to you. Study the techniques and use them to develop a negotiating style that is your own.

Invaluable Pointers to Get You Started

Whether it is your first building or one of many, negotiating the purchase of your investment property requires a variety of skills. At times you may choose to confront the owners directly. In other investments you may use a broker. How you find your properties will determine which negotiating technique you use.

Some real estate investors prefer to drive through various neighborhoods, select certain buildings, and contact the owner to inquire about purchasing.

Instead, you may prefer to scan the real estate ads to see what property is for sale. Again, you may choose to buy from the owner directly or to call one of the many real estate brokers advertising investment property for sale. Still another method is to call a real estate broker you know, give him your preferences and parameters, and let him do the footwork for you. But whatever your method, the following guidelines will get you off to a better start.

1. *Get the facts.* Your main objective in the beginning is to see the building and learn all you can about the property. There is no possible way you can benefit from any dialogue with the seller until you have some basic information about loans, ownership, the number of units, etc.

This is not always an easy task. Brokers hesitate to give addresses over the phone, owners seldom divulge true operating information, and other investors guard their information as if it were gold. Right from the start you will find roadblocks at every corner. But don't be discouraged. Even when people are being very closemouthed, you can learn plenty. For the most part, brokers, sellers, escrow agents, lawyers, moneylenders, and bookkeepers will be looking out for their own interests, not yours, and that is quite natural. The information they give you may be partially complete and accurate or totally in error. You can get the facts you need from these people, but be prepared for a real challenge.

I have negotiated thousands of deals as a buyer, seller, or representative for other individuals and I still go to the negotiation table prepared for real difficulty.

You may wonder about the ideal "win-win" situation. You may have heard the expression "everyone should walk away happy" or "leave a little on the table for the next guy," or even "a deal should be good for both sides." If you believe in any of these concepts, then I would be more than happy to deal with you. Unfortunately, most of the people you will meet across the table are only concerned with "what's in it for me?"

2. *Nobody cares about you but you!* When buying or selling a property you are usually dealing with an individual whom you have never before met and probably will never see again. Do you think he cares about you? His greatest concern is to get the best deal for himself. If he has sold to you and holds an equity position, he does not care if you make a profit, only that you make your payments on time. Should you be late he would not hesitate to foreclose to protect his interest. You are only a buyer or a seller to him, nothing else. You are a means to his end. He will not treat you as he treats his friends or family because you are neither. Remember, in a business deal the only person who cares about you is you.

3. *It pays to be paranoid.* I have often heard people use the phrase "all sellers are liars and all buyers are thieves," and the statement does have some truth. By taking a position that you never trust a buyer if you are the seller and never trust a seller

when you are a buyer, you will never find yourself in trouble with a negative cash-flow property. This theory, which we call "covering your assets," is for your protection.

Never ever accept the seller's information as factual. Do not believe his rent roll, expenses, or even his mortgage payments. Check every figure he gives you, and when you're done, check them again. If you enter each negotiating session with this frame of mind you will be in a better position to protect yourself.

Obviously, a seller will attempt to present his property in the best light possible in order to get the best price. If you realize this and are aware of what can potentially happen, you can save yourself a great deal of time, money, and grief.

Sellers do not limit their "seller enthusiasm" to the novice buyer. When I was an investor in Arizona, I ran into a number of problems with sellers who misstated their utility expenses. Not every buyer is aware that the utilities for apartment buildings can be very high during the 115-degree summer months. When I asked one seller to produce the electricity statements for the previous twelve months, he eagerly provided statements for two meters. Unfortunately, upon inspection of the building, I found three electrical meters, not two.

Another seller gave me the electrical bills for all the meters. When I checked the last twelve months, I discovered two Januarys and two Februarys but no July or August, the two hottest and most expensive months.

Then there was the time when the seller did, in fact, give me statements for each of the twelve months. Further inspection revealed, however, that the bills were two years old! A slight oversight on his part. Especially since utility rates had increased drastically over those two years.

By far the best attempt by a seller to mislead me was in 1977, when he gave me his tax return for 1976 to prove that his utility bill for the year was approximately $10,000. He explained that since it was to his advantage to have high expenses for tax purposes, these figures had to be right. "I would be dumb to put down less and have to pay more taxes," he claimed. Yes he was dumb, dumb as a fox. Knowing he would be selling in 1977 he did not pay his utility bill for November of 1976. In December, he received a bill for two months and then waited until the third of January and paid the bill in full, thereby beating the shut-off date. Now his utility bill for the year 1976 showed $10,000 instead of the true $12,000. We will go into more detail concerning this in a later chapter, but, in essence, showing the $2,000 decrease in his expenses meant an apparent increase in the value of his property of $20,000, at least to the unsuspecting lambs of the world. The cost to the seller was only a delay on the tax write-off, from 1976 to 1977. To quote the Boy Scouts of America, "Be prepared."

4. *He who has the gold, rules.* This is simply the more realistic version of the golden rule. Translated, it means if you have the power, you are in control. However, you do not actually need the power. All you need is for your opponent to *think* you have the power. As in poker, your ability to bluff is very important.

As a syndicator of large apartment complexes I often put together offerings that involve several investors. If the sellers knew that I had to go out and raise the money to purchase the property, they certainly would not be interested in dealing with me. They want someone who has the cash and is able to make a firm commitment. My first job is to impress the seller with my other holdings and let him think I have the cash. I never tell him I have it; I simply let him make his own assumptions.

If, after signing the contract, he finds out that I am going to raise the money, there is nothing he can do about it. The property is mine, at least for several weeks, even months, giving me all the time I need to raise the cash. If I am successful, he also benefits. If I cannot raise the cash (it happened only once), I just exercise my option under the "weasel" clause (explained later in chapter 3, p. 43), and I get my earnest deposit back and go on to the next property. You need the "leading edge"—the power of having, or seeming to have, the gold.

5. *The one who cares the least wins.* This is so simple, yet so important. If you are the buyer and you find a seller who needs to sell, then you have the upper hand. Why? Because he needs the deal more than you do and therefore he is willing to concede more to make the deal. On the other hand, if you have fallen in love with a property, then you need the deal more than the seller and you will be more vulnerable to his terms.

Three years ago my wife and I were in the market for a new home, and she called me at the office to meet her at a house she had just driven by. The realtor showed us in and as we entered the front door the trouble started. All I heard from my wife was, "The carpet is the perfect color for our furniture. The table in the kitchen is exactly what I want. The sunken tennis court is perfect for the kids." This continued throughout the entire tour, with her voice showing more and more excitement, and the realtor showing more and more confidence of an easy sale.

Any chance I had of negotiating a good deal went out the window. The realtor told the seller about my wife's enthusiasm, who immediately took advantage of this edge. Knowing that I wanted the house more than he wanted to sell, he held tight to his price. The result: I bought the house just below full price, but I also asked my wife never to show enthusiasm in front of the opposition.

Did I call the realtor the opposition? Yes I did! Why? Because he is the opposition! Does he care if the seller lowers his price or the buyer raises his? Not one bit! His job is to bring them together and when he does he earns a commission. And this brings to light another premise. There are three sides to each real estate sale: the buyer, the seller, and the broker, each one looking out for himself.

Pedro and the Bandido

Whenever you use a third party to help negotiate, I hope you will remember the story of Pedro and the Bandido.

Seventy years ago in a small Arizona town, a bandido entered the bank, placed his saddlebags on the counter, raised his gun, and demanded that his bags be filled with gold. The teller obliged and the bandido raced to his horse, leaped upon his trusty steed, and headed south to Mexico.

The sheriff formed a posse and headed after the bandido, catching him just before the border. But somehow during the chase the bandido had had time to hide the gold and so he didn't have it with him when apprehended.

Once they had him, they discovered that he did not speak English, and no one in the posse, including the sheriff, spoke Spanish. A member of the posse was sent to town to find a translator. He returned two hours later with a local resident named Pedro.

"Ask him where the gold is!" The sheriff demanded of Pedro.

"Señor, dónde está el oro?" Pedro demanded from the bandido.

"No," the bandido responded. Pedro told the sheriff in broken English, "He does not know, señor."

The sheriff then pointed his shotgun at the bandido and told Pedro, "Tell him to confess where the gold is or I'll blow his head off!"

Pedro rapidly translated in Spanish the sheriff's demand to the confident bandido.

Suddenly the bandido's confidence weakened and he blurted, "El oro está en el pozo!" ("The gold is in the well!")

Pedro then turned to the sheriff, and with a smile interpreted, "Señor Sheriff, the bandido says go ahead and shoot."

Remember, when you're in a negotiation situation be aware

of who is representing you. Be prepared. The only one who will see to it that you keep your gold will be you. Pedro will be looking out for himself.

CHAPTER 2 | Hiring an Agent—the Pros and Cons

Probably the most crucial step you will take is selecting the property. There are a variety of ways to build a real estate empire, but they all begin with the first purchase. Many investors choose a rental house or a small number of residential units. Later, they do some cosmetic work and sell the building at a profit. Of course this really stimulates their interest and, more often than not, their next purchase is a fourplex or larger.

Finding the larger property is not an easy task. The veteran investor has enough experience to minimize his risks and enough connections so that he hears about available properties sooner. The new investor often depends on the advice of the real estate broker to select and negotiate for his first properties. For his smaller investments he might have sought the advice of his local residential broker.

Before long however, the small investor's rental house or duplex grows into five or six units. He then asks himself, "Am I going to rely upon my residential broker to select and negotiate my larger investments?" Until now the small investor may have been content with the services of the residential broker. The rental houses and duplexes were within the broker's area of expertise. Unfortunately, larger income properties are NOT. Eventually you need to move on to a broker who is well versed and experienced in the field of income property investments, or you need to develop this expertise yourself. The sooner you realize this, the sooner you will be able to move forward toward achieving your goals.

How to Pick and Train a Birddog

Let's say your decision is made: You are going to use an income property specialist to handle those investments where a broker is involved. Now you need to pick and train the broker to become a negotiator for you.

Your choice of real estate agent is one of the most important aspects of your making a deal. You will need a lawyer later on, but he should do his thing only—keep you out of trouble. What you need is a good broker or real estate agent. He may or may not be a member of the local board of realtors—there are good and bad agents in both categories.

All Agents Are Not Created Equal

What you want is a specialist with solid experience in the kind of property deals you are looking for. You do not want a residential agent! Their methods and procedures do not lend themselves to investing, and you are not about to buy a house to live in, you are now talking about income property. You need a specialist in this area. You would not go to a dermatologist for an appendectomy, so don't go to a residential agent for income property.

If I had my way there would be different licenses required to sell different types of real estate. One morning I was invited to be the guest speaker at a breakfast sponsored by a local commercial real estate organization. This group of realtors meets weekly to trade ideas, learn about commercial and investment real estate, and possibly put deals together. These meetings, held around the county, are often very productive. But not always. At this particular meeting, a realtor stood during our "haves and wants" session and stated she had a fourplex for sale. She claimed it was a "great buy" because it was "only $25,000 per unit." Yet when a fellow realtor asked her what the cash flow came to, her reply was, "What do you mean by cash flow?"

It is hard to believe that someone had entrusted a $100,000 piece of property to this realtor and was relying on her knowledge and ability. Unfortunately this happens too often!

Remember the story of Pedro and the bandido and don't forget that when you hire an agent, you want to make it worth his or her while to do a good job for *you*. Keep in mind that an agent gets paid only when he brings a buyer and seller together. He gets a commission if the buyer agrees to the seller's price or the seller agrees to the buyer's offer. If neither happens, he gets nothing. Do you think he cares who moves? As a matter of fact, he will receive a higher commission if he gets the seller to raise his offer. Therefore, you are better off choosing one agent to represent you in all your investments, at least in the same area. Let me show you why.

If you have chosen the newspaper as your source of finding a property, you will be calling realtors who have listings (the sellers have let them advertise). Unlike residential real estate, the commercial agent may not have an exclusive right to sell. Anyone can approach the seller directly. However, only when you purchase through the agent will the seller be obligated to pay him a commission.

This being the case, the agent may not give you the address of the property on the phone and will most likely want to meet you and take you to the property. That way he can tell the seller you are his client and the seller will pay a commission if you buy. I do not like to play this way, because I end up dealing with too many brokers and sometimes each of them has the same listings or agreements with the sellers.

In fact, one day I saw the same property advertised in the

Sunday paper by fifteen different real estate offices. Furthermore, each office listed a different price!

When you have your own agent, however, you go through the paper, list the buildings you are interested in, and have him do the footwork to earn his commission. By picking your agent you are saying, "I want you to represent me. In return, you share half of the commission" (the seller's agent will share with him). For this you can expect good representation.

Many of the ads will read "No co-broker" or "principals only," which means that the real estate agent with the listing does not want to split the commission with a privately hired agent. This is his privilege. But it does not hurt to make a call and tell the advertiser the only way that you will be interested in his property is if your agent represents you. If he wants to sell his property, it will be through your agent. Most of the time he will agree that half a pie is better than none.

How to Choose Your Agent in Advance

How do you find a good agent? You can ask friends who have already worked with a particular agent and have been satisfied with their investments. Your attorney or accountant may also be able to steer you toward a good agent. Another alternative is to simply look through the the classified section of the newspaper. Pick an agent whose ads are not outrageous, but look realistic. I had one client who attended a seminar I teach. She figured if I had the ability to get up in front of a class and instruct, I would be a good representative for her.

Set up interviews with several different agents. Ask to talk to them about their services. Remember, you are investing your hard-earned money. Your agent may be the biggest investment of your life. Here is some of the information you want to know:

1. *How long has he been in investment property sales?* Being in real estate as a residential realtor does not count, because the nature of the business is not the same. As I mentioned before, there is more to income property investments than writing an offer, getting acceptance, arranging a bank loan, and closing. Your agent should be experienced and well versed in *commercial income* property investments.

2. *How many investment properties has he been involved in?* Anyone can call himself a commercial agent! Only experience creates good investment agents. Schooling is important, but a good agent with practical experience can make things a lot easier for you.

3. *How many investment properties does the agent own?* If he has experience in the commercial field, he will have his own portfolio. His creativity will have provided him many opportunities along the way to pick up "steals." If he doesn't own any, he does not have the *chutzpah* that I want in an agent. *Chutzpah* is a Yiddish word that does not have an English translation, but "courage," "guts," or "entrepreneurial spirit" come close.

4. *What are his credentials?* There are many fine educational classes available to real estate agents. As in other professions, a better education will allow greater specialization. Look for a C.C.I.M (Certified Commercial Investment Member) or at least a candidate. This series of five week-long courses is designed to educate the agent in the field of income property investment. If the agent has taken a Lowry real estate investment seminar or one similar, he will be able to suggest possible investment alternatives designed especially for the real estate investor. As an instructor for Dr. Lowry's two-day real estate seminar, I have seen both agents and principals with little or no prior knowl-

edge develop a complete understanding of investment real estate in just one immersion weekend. When they work together they make quite a team.

5. *Check his flexibility.* Is the agent and/or broker willing to defer his commission and to take a note or an equity position in lieu of cash? Many deals will hinge on whether the seller needs more cash than you can afford, but with a flexible agent you can create a cushion. For example, if the seller needs $10,-000 down and is asking $20,000 down to compensate for the real estate commission, you can get into the property with $10,000 down if the agents are willing to take the commission in the form of a note.

6. *Will the agent present all offers?* This may sound absurd, but there are many agents who will not "waste the time" presenting all offers. They have predetermined ideas about how contracts are to be written and feel embarrassed to make a "low ball offer." I do not know how many times, after forcing an agent to make an offer, I hear, "My gosh, if I'd thought he would accept that low an offer, I would have bought it myself."

7. *Will he allow me to accompany him on the offers?* Many times I write into the contract the clause that, as purchaser, I have the right to go with the agent on the presentation. This will irritate many agents because they feel threatened. But it is important that I am present. That way, if an item needs to be negotiated or clarified, I am on the spot to do it. It does not have to be relayed through a third party.

The laws in many states require that all offers must be presented. How they are presented is a different story. Offers can be presented, and then they can be *presented!* I want an agent on my side. It will be hard enough dealing with the seller and his agent. I do not need three opponents.

Your agent should meet your needs, not someone else's. Realtors, brokers, agents—all can be extremely valuable to you if they have the knowledge and experience it takes to handle income property transactions. But you are hiring them to work *for* you, not against you. Utilize the talents of a good agent and he may make you more than just a few dollars.

Doing It Yourself

Another alternative available to you is to purchase buildings without a broker or agent. In this case, you will be doing most of the footwork yourself. As I stated in the opening chapter, you may want to drive through the neighborhoods to find "for sale" signs or check your newspaper for buildings that are for sale by owner. These methods require a different skill in the art of negotiating because in each case you will be dealing with a different type of person, in a different type of situation.

THE "FOR SALE" SIGN

As you drive through the neighborhoods you can always find houses that are listed for sale by the owner. Most of these people try to save the real estate commission by selling it themselves. Most likely they have checked with a few friends or called a few real estate agents to get an idea of what their house is worth. Unfortunately, the neighbors they ask often tell their friends and neighbors that they got the full asking price for their homes when in fact they did not. They may be ashamed to admit they took a lesser price. In the end, the "by owner" seller is usually asking top dollar for his property.

Even agents' estimates can be unrealistic. They often use the "PFA" ("Plucked From Air") method of appraisal. The agent appraising the house wants a listing and knows he is in competition with other agents for that listing, so he will naturally give a high price. He knows once he has the listing and no offers come in, he can go back to the client and suggest that the price be lowered to the price that it should have been to start with. As a result, the seller calling an agent for an estimate will often develop an inflated idea on the value of his house.

FIND AN "E.T."

The key is finding an "E.T.," or "easy to"—someone easy to get to see, easy to talk to, easy to negotiate with, and easy to close a deal with. The owner who doesn't have an agent is usually not desperate to sell his house. He probably isn't an E.T. and as a result you may have some trouble in this case. You will want to find out his "hot button" or why he needs to sell his house, but he will not likely be about to tell you what his real reason is. It could be a job transfer to a new city, a divorce, having to make two payments on two different houses, or any number of other reasons. Obviously the more drastic the reason, the easier it is for you to negotiate. During your conversations with the seller you will have different opportunities to ask the reason for selling. If you ask often enough and do it in different ways, you will be able to piece together the real reason. Some questions that may be able to help you out are: "When do you have to be out?" "What do you need the down payment for?" "Are you going to stay until the kids finish the school year?"

Some buyers stop by a prospective house at about four o'-clock in the afternoon, when the parents are still working and the kids are home, to ask them the reason their parents are selling, although you risk offending the seller with this technique.

THE MULTIPLE LISTING BOOK

The M.L.S. (Multiple Listing) book is another method for finding E.T.'s. This book is published, usually weekly, by the various boards of realtors throughout the country. It shows all the current property for sale. There is no edge in having the current book. The trick to finding the "easy to" sellers is to get a book that is about six months old and compare it to one from last month. If you see a property still in the book you know you have a worried seller. He is now ready to negotiate. One friend of mine makes a living by offering 25 percent below market price on any listing more than four months old.

FORECLOSURES AND SHERIFF SALES

These sales are another source of good properties that require the ability to negotiate. We will spend more time on the specifics of foreclosures later in the book, but for now consider that most people facing foreclosure are anxious to negotiate. The problem most people run into when negotiating with people who are about to lose their property is that they worry that they will "step on a person" who is down. In fact, you are helping such people get out of trouble. It should not be difficult to convince the seller that you are saving his credit rating and giving him something on his property when he was about to wind up with nothing.

DON'T FORGET THE FARM

One of the least-known ways to find a property by yourself is the "farming system," which is used by many real estate agents. You go to a local title company and ask them for a "farm kit" for a certain neighborhood that you have driven through and feel is the right area for a purchase.

The title company will check the public tax records and come up with the names, addresses, and many times the telephone numbers of all the property owners in the neighborhood. They will also supply you with the price and terms of each of their purchases. And all of this just for asking!

Take the Fear out of Contracts

Educated Risks

You may not feel you are quite ready to learn about real estate contracts, but I want you to have the information now so that you realize how simple they really are. You are reading this book because you are planning to invest what seems like a lot of money in a new home, apartment building, land, or commercial property. You are looking for help and may be quite worried about making the first offer to purchase. You aren't sure how the whole process works and are plagued by the fear that you will make a terrible mistake.

Although there is no guarantee that every deal will make you a fortune, there is a method that will give you the time you need to give it your best shot. That is what this chapter is all about: the "all-inclusive weasel clause."

The All-Inclusive Weasel Clause

How many times have you made quick decisions and then discovered that you acted too hastily? How many times have you asked yourself, "Why didn't I sleep on it?" or better yet, "Why didn't I check it out first?" Now you can, by simply using the all-inclusive weasel clause. This clause will give you up to five weeks to check the property over and have your attorney read the purchase contract, yet at the same time it ties up the property so no one else can purchase it. Furthermore, you can do it without spending one single dime of your own.

To be most effective, the clause must be worded exactly as you see it here:

> This offer contingent upon receipt and approval of all books, records, leases, personal management contracts, preliminary title report, underlying encumbrances, and physical inspection of the property. Purchaser to have fourteen working days from receipt of above to remove all contingencies in writing or this contract is null and void and all monies to be returned in full.

Always place the all-inclusive weasel clause in your contract to purchase. If you use a real estate broker's purchase contract, it may already have blank spaces for such clauses. This will protect you against unscrupulous sellers who lay traps for the unwary.

Tie the Property Up so You Can Do Your Homework

Now you will have tied up the property for several weeks so that you can do your homework. For example, let us say that you see a nice little sixplex you think would be good for you. You want to tie it up immediately because properties that good do not come along too often. On the surface this one appears to have great investment potential. What can you do to tie it up without fully obligating yourself? Here's how I used the weasel clause to my advantage not long ago.

I found a house in Michigan with potential for conversion into a seven-room boardinghouse. At the time I found it, a couple was living in the house with their three children. He was being transferred and was a classic "E.T." He needed out and was willing to take nothing as a down payment and offer good terms.

After looking it over, I believed I had a good property, so I sat down on the spot, took out a "standard" contract, and wrote an offer to purchase. We spent the next hour or so negotiating, and when I left, I had a signed contract. Naturally, I included my all-inclusive weasel clause in the contract, so I was safe. It enabled me to take all the time I needed to inspect the roof, electrical wiring, heating, air-conditioning, mortgages, and anything else I desired.

Later that same day, feeling satisfied about the purchase, I drove my wife to the site to see our investment. Not finding the seller at home dampened my enthusiasm, but only momentarily. We walked through the site, and as we returned to the car three men arrived asking if I knew where the owner was. I told them I was the new owner. The spokesman for the three looked shocked. He explained that he had seen the property last week and had come back with his partners so they could see it. If they liked it, they were going to make an offer. I told them I had not closed escrow yet, but would be happy to sell my position for a profit. Of course this didn't go over too well and they left empty-handed.

They had patience, and ended up with nothing. If the first partner had made an offer that tied the property up as I had, he could have had the property if he had wanted it, and he could have backed out later if his partners hadn't liked it.

You cannot have patience and expect to be successful in real estate. You need the *chutzpah* to move quickly. However, you also need the escape clause to get out if after doing your homework, you decide that you shouldn't go ahead with the purchase.

The Key Word Is "Approval"

The wording in the weasel clause is *very* important. A friend of mine left out the words "and approval" and the seller insisted that he did not have the right of approval, just the right to review the information. As a result, he had to complete the transaction. Later on, the court did rule in favor of my friend, but it took one year and legal fees to close the case. Please do not forget the words "and approval."

When you have a properly worded weasel clause you actually have *five weeks* to decide! The seller had one goal in mind as he read your offer: to sell his six units for the best price and terms. The average seller is more concerned with price and terms than anything else in the contract. This is quite normal. Chances are if you wrote the offer properly he will not accept your first offer and will make a counter-offer. He will be so concerned with the price and terms that he will tend to bypass minor items. It's sort of like the "major-minor" close that salesmen have been using effectively for years. By distracting the seller with one item, the other items go by without careful scrutiny. This is why we worded the clause exactly as we did. We want the seller to read the contract, but only to focus on certain items. This is how the strategy works.

He will see the fourteen days, but will probably not notice the word "working." Read the following and test yourself:

> Now is the time
> for all good men
> to come to the
> the aid of their
> party.

Not many of you spotted the two "the" 's right after one another, did you? You saw a paragraph you were used to seeing and did not bother to read it carefully. Fourteen days means two weeks, but fourteen *working* days means one day less than *three* weeks.

The seller, being anxious to close, does not realize that the words "from receipt of the above" means the clock does not start until all these requested items are delivered. He thinks that it is two weeks from the day he accepts the offer. It should take a minimum of two weeks to get all the information. Sometimes it takes months.

On January 21, 1982, I made an offer with my partner Steve Wallace to purchase an office building. Although it was accepted the same day with the all-inclusive weasel clause, it was the sixth of April before we finally received the last document. With the additional fourteen working days we had until April 26 to raise the money for the project. There had been no risk on our part, and we had tied the property up for thirteen weeks while we raised the funds necessary to complete the deal, and everybody, including the seller, finally came out a winner.

As you can see the all-inclusive weasel clause enables you to buy extra time to gather the facts and funds necessary for a sound purchase. Include it in all your contracts—it will save you more than a few headaches.

Deposit Check Clause

Another clause that should be included in your purchase contract is the "deposit check clause." It allows you to make several offers on different buildings without having to come up with the cash that a seller usually wants as earnest money. Earnest money is a deposit that most sellers ask for along with the offer to show that the buyer is acting in good faith and really wants to purchase the property. However, if you stop to think about it, earnest money doesn't make much sense. Let me explain.

Every contract has a line on which we list the company to which we are paying the earnest money deposit. (Never give it directly to the seller; it could take months to get it back.) Directly after the name of the company, write your "deposit check clause," which reads: "to be deposited upon removal of contingencies." With this line, you have now given a check that *cannot* be cashed until you write a letter that removes the contingencies spelled out in your all-inclusive weasel clause. As a result, you have at least five weeks before you need the cash to cover the check.

If there is a contingency clause in the contract and the purchaser decides not to go through with the deal, he is entitled to the money back anyway. So it makes little sense for the seller to collect the money, have it deposited, open an escrow account, and cause the real estate broker to go through all the paperwork before the contingencies are removed and the buyer is ready to proceed.

There will even be times when the contingencies have been removed and the buyer still ends up with his money back if he wants out.

I sold a forty-unit apartment complex and had a $10,000 earnest money check deposited with an escrow company. The closing date came and went, and the buyer did not close. After many conversations I discovered that the buyer could not come up with the balance of the down payment.

Finally, with another offer in hand, I wrote to both the buyer and the escrow company canceling the deal and requesting the earnest money on account of his failure to complete the deal.

Although I was legally entitled to the deposit, I never collected it because I received a letter from the buyer's attorney stating that they would contest the payment in court. He also told me that even if I did win the case, it would take at least one year to get the money and my property would be tied up during that time. Principle is one thing, but I needed a sale at the time, so I released the money and sold the building to a new buyer. Ever since that day, I take earnest money for what it is worth: NOTHING. As long as it is valued as nothing, why should we tie up our money?

Do Not Let the Broker Persuade You to Leave the Clause Out

Most states have laws requiring the broker or escrow company to deposit all earnest money checks within one or two business days after the receipt of the check. However, this law applies *only when the contract does not specifically contradict that law.* If both parties agree to waive this deposit through a deposit check clause as shown above, then the broker or escrow company is relieved of the legal obligation to deposit the check.

Unfortunately, most brokers don't know this. If you get in an argument about the deposit, do not give in! Remember, most agents are accustomed to writing contracts only one way. When they are asked to deviate from the norm, they are often confused because they are not aware of the alternatives.

If the agent does not mention your clause to the seller, don't bring it to his attention. It is his duty to mention it to the seller, not yours. The less conflict you create, the easier the negotiations will go. However, after you have the signed contract in hand, do remind the agent of the clause because you don't want him to deposit the check inadvertently.

Last year, after getting a contract accepted, I reminded the agent of the five-week hold on the check. Upon reading my "standard" clause (he didn't believe me), he stated that he would have to go back to the seller and tell him, and offer him the opportunity to back out. He also felt the clause was illegal. Neither was true. He checked with the state real estate commissioner and found out from his attorney that the seller had signed the contract and had to abide by the terms. The only person in trouble was the agent—for not reading the contract carefully and informing the seller about all the terms.

During my lectures I am often asked if I would accept a weasel clause in a contract if I were the seller, and whether the seller's attorney would allow him to accept such a clause.

In the last twelve years, I have written many contracts for myself and for my clients as buyers. There has been a weasel clause in *every* contract. I will not write a contract without it, and should the seller not accept it, I go on to another building.

Would I accept such a clause? Let me preface the answer by acknowledging that I am a tough negotiator, as you will be after you have mastered the skills explained in later chapters. But, I have accepted weasel clauses when I have sold properties. If a person is a prospective buyer, I want to do everything possible to help him buy my property. Since he can get the earnest money deposit back anyway, I don't bother asking for it. But the weasel clause is *not* an underhanded measure. It is simply a way of buying time *without* spending money until you have enough information on a property to make a good decision.

The Weasel Clause and You as the Seller

As a seller I have also found ways to circumvent the weasel clause. One time, when selling an eighteen-unit apartment, I made out escrow instructions, signed them, and produced a package with the leases, rent, underlyings, title report, and income statements. I gave this package to any person requesting it with the following instructions, "Go and visit the building, check out all the figures, and if you're the first person to sign the escrow instructions, you get the property." Five days later I had a signed contract, and two weeks after that we closed escrow. This method broke the traditional way of selling, but did accomplish two things. First, it motivated people to do the inspections quickly, and second, it didn't allow one person to tie up my property so that I would lose other buyers.

The alternative to this is to put into the counter-offer an "anti-weasel clause." That goes right after the buyer's weasel clause. Following the words "and all money returned in full" add, "However, should the seller receive a firm offer, he may, at his option, give written notice to the purchaser to remove all contingencies in writing within forty-eight hours of receipt of notice or this offer becomes null and void and all earnest money is to be returned in full."

By adding the anti-weasel clause I take away the buyer's right to tie up the property for five weeks. If I find another "live buyer" I reduce it to two days. If I don't, I'll let the buyer think he has the best of me and let him "tie" it up for weeks. Keep in mind the fact that if you let the opposition think they have won a battle, the next one will be easier for you.

A Check Is Money Only When It Is Cashed

Each time I add the check deposit clause, I think of the story of the rabbi, minister, and priest.

Once there were three religious leaders called to the bedside of an eccentric millionaire, who very weakly requested, "Since you are all trusted men of the cloth, I am entrusting you with envelopes containing $1 million each. At the time of my death I want each of you to pass my coffin and drop the money in so that I will take it with me when I die so my relatives will never discover where it went."

Within a week he was dead and each religious leader passed

by the coffin and, as instructed, dropped an envelope into the coffin.

One year later, the three met and the minister sheepishly confessed that he had taken his million dollars and placed an empty envelope into the coffin. He needed the money to give his poor, underprivileged congregation their first Christmas.

The rabbi and priest both told him that he should not feel bad since he was doing the work of God. "As a matter of fact," said the priest, "I too placed an empty envelope in the coffin." He continued by saying, "As you know I had a church that was falling apart, had no heat, and was plagued with a leaky roof. I spent the money on a new church."

Both the rabbi and the minister relieved him of his guilty feelings since he too was doing the work of God.

Being the rabbi's turn to speak, the priest and minister stared at him and finally asked, "Rabbi, did you really put the money in the coffin as you were instructed?"

"But of course," said the rabbi. "And just to make sure it was safe, I took the cash out and put my own personal check in for $1 million."

Your check is as safe as the rabbi's if you write your contract properly.

Now that you are comfortably set with the all-inclusive weasel clause, you can go out and make your first offer. Don't worry about making a mistake or getting into trouble. You have five weeks to cancel the deal, simply by not removing your contingencies.

With that in mind let's go on to writing the contract.

Even Your Name Is Negotiable

The first line on the purchase contract calls for the name of the individual making the offer. This is probably the most neglected item on the contract. It can be the source of excellent negotiation opportunities but it gets the least attention. All too often buyers arbitrarily fill in their name and proceed to the remaining parts of the contract. But, as you will see in this chapter, even your name is a negotiable item on the contract. By simply following your name with the words "and/or nominee" you may save yourself a great deal of time, money, and aggravation. In essence, the "and/or nominee" addition eliminates your need to negotiate with the seller should you find an individual who wishes to purchase the property you have offered on but not yet closed.

Not long ago, for example, I offered to purchase sixty-five new patio homes from a developer. On each contract I negotiated a wholesale price using the "and/or nominee" clause. Of the sixty-five homes, forty-one had not even closed escrow before I had a purchaser for them. You see, each time the builder completed a unit I found a buyer and substituted his/her name for mine under the "and/or nominee" provision. The purchaser paid me the difference between my purchase price and my sales price and I "nominated" him to step into my shoes on the contract. Obviously, the builder would have preferred to sell the homes directly to my purchasers, but was prevented from doing so by my "and/or nominee" clause.

When he discovered the kind of profit he was missing out on, he attempted to make me close each deal, qualify for each loan, and pay all the appraisal fees, back fees, and title policies before I could sell any to my buyers. Thanks to the "and/or nominee" clause he was legally required to allow me to sell to my nominee. Then as a last resort he offered to compromise and split the profits with me. Fortunately, he had nothing to negotiate with, since the "and/or nominee" clause had taken away all of his power to negotiate and had given it to me.

The "and/or nominee" clause does the seller no real harm and is perfectly legitimate. After all, he made all his sales at the agreed-upon price. You are under no real obligation to explain anything, but the seller may nevertheless raise some objections. What happens if the seller you're working with questions the use of the "and/or nominee" statement? Try one of these answers. They usually will work for me.

1. "I'm not sure if I am going to purchase this with my spouse or in my name alone."
2. "My attorney may want me to put the title into a trust."
3. "I have not formed my partnership yet, so I don't have a name for it."

Never Give Money to the Seller

The next item on the contract is always the earnest money, an amount which, by tradition, goes to the seller or his agent as a sign of good faith. Essentially it shows that you want to go through with the transaction.

As we discussed earlier, your deposit amount should be followed by the "to be deposited upon removal of contingencies" clause. However, this may not work every time. What about the occasion when the seller insists upon receiving something up front? In this case, be sure to find a neutral third party to hold the funds. In many states you will be using an escrow company to close the sale and finalize your purchase. If you do use an escrow company, make your deposit check out to that company. Another alternative is to make the deposit check out to a real estate company if you are going through one. *Under no circumstances should you give the deposit to the seller!* Real estate companies and escrow companies are regulated by state agencies and are required to hold all deposit funds in a trust account. If you fail to remove the contingencies in the alloted time period and request a return of your deposit, these companies will give it back to you without delay once you have pointed out the fact that the contract is null and void and all earnest money is to be returned in full.

This is not the case when the seller is given the deposit directly. If the deal doesn't go through, you may have trouble getting your deposit back. He is probably going to be angry since he believed the deal would close and has already made plans for spending the money. He may have felt you were not being fair with him and wants to teach you a lesson by keeping your money. If you have written the contract properly, you will get the money back eventually, provided the seller still has it. But it may take you a while and cost you unnecessary legal fees.

A client of mine, whom I'll call Mr. Thompson, made the mistake of paying his deposit directly to the seller, and suffered for it. A landscaper had purchased a home from a builder and had given the builder $2,000 as an earnest deposit, with the balance to be due when the house was completed. Time passed and the value of the property increased each month the house stood incomplete. As a result, the landscaper saw an opportunity to make an $8,000 profit by selling his contract to Mr. Thompson. Likewise, Mr. Thompson, with the passage of time, saw an additional $10,000 profit when the house was completed.

Mr. Thompson agreed to purchase the property subject to the landscaper's ability to deliver under the agreed-upon terms. Mr. Thompson also agreed to write the landscaper a check for the $2,000 he had paid out of his pocket, believing that the profit would come in when he sold the house. He had committed a cardinal sin. The builder never turned the house over to the landscaper, claiming inflated costs, and thereby allowing him to back out under his own weasel clause. The builder returned the $2,000 deposit to the landscaper. Unfortunately, the landscaper proceeded to spend it as soon as he received it, and there was no money for Mr. Thompson by the time he discovered the deal was off.

Two years later, the court awarded Mr. Thompson $2,000 along with an additional $1,100 in legal fees he had had to pay out to get it back. Yet, Mr. Thompson's $3,100 was tied up for two years because he made the foolish mistake of giving the seller the earnest deposit.

CHAPTER
4 | # The Right Price

The price is possibly the most sensitive, widely negotiated item in any real estate contract. To many buyers and sellers, the selling price of a property is very important. Let's explore how to come up with a "right price."

You Make Money When You Buy Real Estate

As a realtor, I talk to a great many sellers. One of the most common problems they share is not getting enough for their property when it is sold. Either they complain because they did not get enough cash at close of escrow, or they are unhappy with the terms of the financing. Overall, the story is the same: They end up taking much less than the listing agent said the property was worth.

There is an expression in the real estate business which you should be aware of: "A good selling agent can make a lot of money if he works smart." Once a listing agent has a pocketful of listings, he is going to reap the rewards because he gets a commission on all the sales, whether he closes the deal or not. He has all the other real estate agents working for him selling his listings. Crafty listing agents overprice your property to get the listing and then will get you to lower your price later, by blaming the economy, the market, the President, the banks, and everyone else. The fact is, someone will pay you only what your property is worth. Sometimes you may find a

The money is made at the buy

"dummy" willing to pay you a premium, but don't hold your breath.

Usually the best road to successful real estate investing is to start by buying a building at below-market value. Negotiate the price and terms so that if you had to sell the building tomorrow you could still make a profit. In my experience that has been an important element in the big profits in real estate. One investor I know of stated this concept quite well. "When I buy real estate, I know exactly how much money I'll make on the building before I even close escrow. That's because I make my money buying at a reasonable price, not selling at a higher price."

In order to make money, you must buy the property at a good price so that you can sell it for a profit.

What Is the Right Price?

There is rarely one "right price." You and I could be buying the same property and the right price could be any of ten different figures. The right price depends on several things. There are four items in a contract that are interrelated with one another:

1. Price
2. Down payment
3. Interest rate
4. Time period

The terms of the contract play an important role in establishing the "right price."

Under normal negotiations, the price will be lower as the down payment increases and other terms become better for the seller. Conversely, the price will increase when the down payment is lowered, and the terms become more favorable to the buyer.

Getting Your Offer Accepted so You Can Start
Negotiations

There are two stages to getting a contract accepted. The first stage is to get the seller to believe you are really interested, in order to see his books, records, and all the other items set forth in the weasel clause, and to have a physical inspection of the building. Therefore you will make an initial offer to show your interest in the property. The second stage is submitting your real offer after examining the records and the building.

Based on the premise that "all sellers are liars," any information you are given prior to our inspection is going to be "wrong." Chapter 5 will deal with the formulas you can use to check and verify the seller's numbers. For now, let's concentrate on the method you will use to make your initial and real offers.

The real offer, after the inspections, will be *lower* than the initial one. If it is too much lower you will be running the risk of insulting the seller, or worse yet, making him an offer he cannot live with. To prevent such problems, you will have to make your initial offer as realistic as possible. At the same time, you do not want to make an initial offer that is totally acceptable to the buyer (such as full price and terms), only to see the books and realize your real offer will be too far off.

Thus, your first purchase contract should be negotiated in such a way that if all the information supplied to you from the seller is correct, you will be willing to complete the deal. This way, if any of the seller's information is incorrect, you will have a logical reason to make your second offer lower. The real offer is based on corrected information, but worked out by the same guidelines and formulas.

The Gross Rent Multiplier and the Net Rent Multiplier

In order to make reasonable offers to purchase, you will need to understand two simple but very important factors—the annual *Gross* Rent Multiplier (GRM) and the annual *Net* Rent Multiplier (NRM)—and the formulas used to arrive at them.

The GRM is a figure you create as a rough guideline for comparing properties, and is also used for formulating your initial offer. The GRM varies according to location, age of the building, etc., and is usually derived by comparing the annual rent rolls (annual gross rent on a building, not allowing for any vacancies) plus other income from the building with the selling prices of buildings of the same type sold recently in the same locale. In your initial contract negotiation, you will temporarily have to accept the seller's word for these figures (since, needless to say, you do not want to waste your time if your price range does not agree with the seller's).

To get the value based on the GRM you multiply the annual gross income by the multiplier that you will determine. (See below.) The resulting total will be your initial offer.

The NRM is also a number that you create and that you will multiply by the actual annual net rent figure supplied by the seller to arrive at a purchase offer. This multiplier is somewhat harder to derive since it is based on the seller's real income minus expenses.

You will use the value from the GRM in the preliminary contract only; it can be dispensed with when you get down to the real negotiations. The value from the NRM will be your guideline in the final phases of the contract negotiations. In order to use these formulas, you will first have to know how to determine the multipliers.

DETERMINING THE GROSS RENT MULTIPLIER

Whether you use the Gross Rent Multiplier or the Net Rent Multiplier, the number you create must make sense to both the buyer and the seller (so he doesn't feel he is selling too cheaply). It is based on the type of building you want to buy and the area in which you are looking.

To find the GRM and to find a reasonable offering price, first you must determine what other buildings have sold for in the area. Then divide the average cost of the buildings sold by the annual gross income. The resulting figure is the GRM. Remember, each city, neighborhood, and type of building has its own special set of circumstances which will affect your calculations. Therefore, you must derive the number methodically each time you are looking at a prospective purchase. The most important factors to be aware of are supply and demand, although location, age, economic climate, amenities, and even the reputation of the building will also have an influence on the value and hence the multiplier. If there are more buyers than there are sellers for a specific type of property, the sellers will be able to raise their prices and your multiplier will go up. On the other hand, if there are more sellers than buyers, prices will come down, as will the multiplier. The lowering of the multiplier shows a softening in the marketplace, and you should be aware that although you will be able to buy the property more cheaply, there are fewer buyers interested and you should try to find out why.

For example, let's say you find that buildings similar to the one you want to buy have recently sold for $300,000. The annual gross rents have averaged $30,000. Thus, the GRM for that type of building in that area is 10.

Price		Income		GRM
$300,000	/	30,000		= 10

If a $90,000 building had an annual gross income of $10,000 the GRM would be 9.

$$\$90,000 \ / \ 10,000 = 9$$

The lower the GRM, the better the buy, provided the properties are equal in all other respects. The lower the GRM, the lower the purchase price for the same income.

DETERMINING THE NET RENT MULTIPLIER

The NRM must be used for calculating your final purchase offer. It is based on the much more accurate and realistic figure you will have after inspecting the building and reviewing the present owner's actual records.

To determine the NRM, then, you will need to find out the real figures, or the Net Operating Income (NOI) of that particular building. Then you will divide the price by the NOI, and the result is the NRM. Remember, you should still use the price you have arrived at by comparing similar buildings in the same area—never use the seller's asking price in your calculations.

To determine the NOI you first add *all* the annual income for a specific property (rent, vending machines, parking, laundry, etc.). Then, from this total you subtract all expenses and a carefully estimated amount for vacancy. When figuring the NOI do not include amounts for debt service, which is the mortgage payment or the payment on the land contract, trust, deed, agreement for sale, or any other method of paying off the encumbrance of the property. (Another name for NOI is "Net Before Debt," since it does not consider the mortgage or encumbrance.)

Once you have determined the NOI you then multiply it by your NRM and a value is obtained. Use the NRM based on a price that you have determined is fair for that area and that type of building. For example, if the NOI is $30,000 and the NRM for the area is 10, the value for the building is $300,000.

Let's take a more detailed example. Two fourplexes (A & B) are next door to each other and were built by the same builder at the same time. Their apartments are identical, and in fact everything about the buildings is the same except that in A, the builder installed one central heating and air-conditioning unit, and in B separate units were installed in each apartment, allowing tenants to pay their own utilities.

After doing your research in the marketplace, you find that similar apartment units have sold for $120,000 to $130,000 over the last six months in the same neighborhood.

Let's work out the different numbers:

	Building A		Building B
1.	$12,000	Rent $250 × 4 units × 12	$12,000
2.	+1,000	Other income	+1,000
3.	$13,000	Gross Income	$13,000
4.	−650	Vacancy	−650
5.	$12,350	Adjusted gross income	$12,350
6.	−5,000	Expenses	−2,000
7.	$7,350	Net Operating Income	$10,350

If the sellers of these two buildings were each asking $130,000 for them, the Gross Rent Multiplier on each one would be 10 (obtained by dividing the asking price by the gross income). If, on the other hand, the buyer could get the seller to sell for $110,000, the GRM would be lowered to about 8½ ($110,000, divided by gross income). Remember, the lower the GRM the better the value, as long as everything else is equal.

Initially, these two buildings appear equal in value, but there is a major factor not considered when using the GRM but which comes into play when figuring the NRM. Because the owner of building A has to pay the utilities, he has only $7,350 left for mortgage payments and profits (line 7), while the owner of building B (whose tenants pay utilities) has more than $10,000 left for mortgage payments and profits. This discrepancy becomes clear when we calculate the NRM on each building (by dividing the price by the NOI). At the $130,000 price, the NRM on building A would be 17.7, while the NRM on building B would be 12.5. Obviously the lower the NRM, the better the deal for the buyer, because the lower the NRM, the higher the profit.

HOW TO GET THE INFORMATION YOU WILL NEED

The best way to determine the multiplier for a specific property is to start with the newspaper. Call the ads in the classified section and ask for the price, the rent roll, and the expenses on as many buildings as possible. Calculate the GRM and NRM for each, based on their information and prices even though you know the final multipliers will be different.

Now drive around the neighborhoods. Check out the properties similar to the one you want to buy. They should be as close as possible in age, style, type, and size. While you are out, watch for any amenities, such as a pool, covered parking, game or recreation rooms, and proximity to bus lines, schools, and shopping centers. Ask tenants or superintendents who pays utilities (the owner or the tenant), and what extra amenities, such as cable television and day-care centers, are offered.

Next, check with your local real estate agent and see if any of these properties have been sold recently. Find out as much as you can about the selling prices and other details of the sales. If the agent cannot help, head for the local county recorder's office to check for recent sales records on the properties. Also, shop for an apartment or office space to find out the rental rates in the area. You will need this figure once you have the selling prices of the area to help you determine what you will charge to rent your building.

Then, with the sales, income, and expense information, you can easily establish both a correct GRM and a correct NRM to use in evaluating the property.

Since the valuations using the GRM and the NRM are based on properties in the general area that were negotiated by people who aren't as smart as you, adjust the price downward based on the fact that you will be negotiating with an "E.T.," who has more reason to sell than you have to buy. If your offer is not what the seller wants, then be prepared to walk away and make an offer on another building. One day, one week, even one month is not going to hurt you or your long-range investment goals. There will always be people willing to sell at your price and terms. It is important to base your adjustments to your price and terms on the premise of "He who cares the least wins."

Always Buy on the Basis of a Need to Sell Tomorrow

Although you are buying to make a profit, you never know when an emergency may come up. You may need money for a "deal of a lifetime" investment, or you may have financial difficulties and need cash to operate. Whatever the reason, you must be prepared to sell the property tomorrow. Remember, since you never want to suffer a loss, *you must buy at a price far enough below market price to be able to sell, pay a commission, and still break even.*

You Really Can Buy Cheap

By now you are probably scratching your head thinking, "This guy is wacky! No one is going to sell at prices so far under the market." But if that were so, neither I nor anyone else would own very much property today. Let me give you a classic example of this "buy low" concept. In 1978, I made an offer of $595,000 for a twenty-four-unit apartment building and was turned down flat. Actually I started at $535,000 and came up to $595,000, which was the price I was willing to pay. The seller, starting at $730,000, would not budge below $650,000. No deal was made. Six months later, through a reliable source, I learned that the seller was in a bad financial position with the building. The resident manager had quit, the property management company was not doing a good job, and the building was becoming run-down. The seller meanwhile was located in another state and was unaware of the problems.

It took only a phone call to the seller and a few follow-up photographs to convince him to sell. This time we ended up at $585,000 ($10,000 less than my original final offer)!

A deal on a smaller scale involved a duplex located in Arizona. The seller needed cash right away for other ventures already contracted and sold his property for $41,000. The buyer qualified for a new 95 percent mortgage guarantee insurance corporation loan, so the seller could get his cash out. The buyer had to use only $12,000 of his own money. The best part of this deal happened one month later when the buyer sold the duplex for what it was really worth, $48,000. Because he negotiated from strength, he realized a comfortable $7,000 profit in a very short time.

You too can make $7,000 on a $2,000 investment in one month. And if you have the *chutzpah* to walk away until a deal suits you, you can do even better. Believe me, the deals are out there, just waiting for you to create them!

Keeping Sellers Honest

Since so many of our decisions to buy are based on net operating income, it is important to have a correct figure for the NOI.

Any error in the NOI *is magnified to a very costly size.* For example, if the net rent multiplier is 10, an NOI off by $1,000 would result in an error of $10,000 in the purchase price.

Figuring the Net Operating Income

Let us examine a practical example. Apartments in a twenty-unit building are actually renting monthly for $225 each, but the seller leads us to believe the rent is $250 per unit. Multiply this $25 difference by each unit and you have $500 per month or $6,000 per year less in income. Using 10 as our net rent multiplier, the building would have a $60,000 lower actual value than our figure for the NOI, and we would be looking at a property that we could not sell until we increased the rent roll.

You can also run up against the same type of problem when you consider expenses. If you happen to leave out the gardening expense, short the taxes and insurance, or delete the advertising cost because you were not informed of these expenses, before you know it, you will be paying $20,000, $30,000, or even more above the true value of the building.

To avoid such costly errors you need a set of guidelines to help keep the seller honest.

Keeping track of the following list of factors has been enormously helpful with many of my purchases. It may take some work, but you will not be wasting time. Should you not do it, you will be risking much more than time; you run the risk of wasting a lot of money!

When negotiating your first offer and counter-offer, you will not need to go through the elaborate list described. Accept the seller's numbers at face value and just use the formula:

INCOME

	Rent	= $
+	Laundry	= $
+	Vending machines	= $
+	Other	= $
=	Gross rent	= $
−	Vacancy	= $
=	Adjusted gross rent	= $
−	Expenses	= $
=	Net operating income	= $

Be sure that during your negotiations you make the seller aware that you are basing all your offers on the facts he has provided and should there be a deviation (which has never failed to happen) the offer will change. This opens the door for the real negotiations.

Rent

There are only two ways to be positive the rent roll is correct. One is to check the leases or rental agreements; the other is to get a signed letter from each tenant. DO NOT accept any other method. It is too easy to doctor a receipt book, bank account, or even I.R.S. returns.

Your first choice is to study the leases or rental agreements. Whether there are four units or two hundred, you must read each one of them and you must read every page.

All too often, I have seen sellers give away a free month's rent for a twelve-month lease in an effort to show a full building. Which month do you think is free? Right, the *last* month, the one YOU will have to give away. Not only will you not get the rent for that month, but the true value of the building is lower than you expected. If the lease calls for eleven payments of $250 for a twelve-month period, then the true rent is only $229 per month over a one-year period and is only what that building in that neighborhood will rent for. If you deduct $21 per unit per month and multiply by twelve months, and multiply that figure by twenty (for a twenty-unit building), the value could decrease by $60,000. Remember, if there are leases when you purchase a building, you must abide by those leases. Note the advanced rent and deposits paid by the seller plus any unusual fees such as key fees or pet deposits. You will be liable to return these when the tenant moves out. If the seller has collected for these he should turn them over to you at closing, and will, but only if you have asked for such monies in your contract. Do not leave it to negotiation at the closing.

When you run into the seller who has no leases and no rental agreements (everything is month to month on a handshake)—and you will—then, prior to removal of your weasel clause, you must ask for a signed letter from each tenant stating his monthly rent, deposits, and any advance monies or extras he has given the seller. It should also state through what date the rent has been paid and on what day it is due, and when the tenant moved in. The following example is a good one to use:

Sample Letter

I _____, residing at _____, apt. #____

   (NAME)   (ADDRESS)

_____, am paying rent at the rate of $____

(CITY, STATE, ZIP)

per month, and I am paid through _____, 19____.

I moved in on _____, 19____.

I have a refundable security deposit of $_____, on deposit with the owner. I have no other monies on deposit.

Dated this ____ day of _____, 19____.

_____

(SIGNATURE OF TENANT)

    The tenant's move-in day is important for two reasons. If the building is a transient building, it will have a higher vacancy factor and a higher maintenance factor, thus lowering the value of the property. If you are considering a transient property you could also be looking at a "stacked building," one in which the seller stacks the building with free or near-free tenants to show the building as full.

    I purchased a forty-unit apartment building in Tucson, Arizona, and read each rental agreement. However, I neglected to check the move-in dates. The building had a more than 95 percent occupancy level, but one month after I owned the building, we were down to 70 percent. Seven tenants, who had been there less than two months, had moved out. We could never prove it, but from talking to the people who left and other tenants, we believe the seller had "stacked" the building to show it in a better light. *Always* check those leases carefully!

Other Income

Rent is not the only source of income in an apartment building or a single family home. Many owners will not record other
income because much of it is cash and they pocket it to save on
taxes. Not only is this illegal skimming, it is foolish. On the
basis of what you have already learned, $20 a month in the
landlord's pocket is $240 per year in undeclared income and
therefore at least $2,400 off the asking price.

Other income can include laundry, security deposits, parking
fees, pet deposits, key charges, and late charges. However, laundry and deposits should be listed separately. Unless the seller
can prove that deposits are a constant source of income rather
than a one-time arrangement, you should not use them in your
calculations for NOI. Consider them your bonus for buying the
building. There will always be unexpected expenses and this
additional money can help offset them.

LAUNDRY

When you figure income from laundry you can use one of two
methods. Use either the figure from the seller or the following
formula, whichever is more advantageous to you.

Whether people live in New York, Milwaukee, Phoenix, or
L.A., they are going to get their clothes dirty. Generally they
get just as dirty wherever they are.

Figure on $3 per unit per month for laundry income if you
are renting machines, and double that if you own them, or use
the seller's numbers if his are less. However, if he has skimmed
off the laundry money it will be difficult for him to verify this
income.

There are many companies that will lease laundry machines
to you and split the profit. It is a very simple and desirable

arrangement. The company will take care of the maintenance and replacement and you will be responsible for the electricity and water bills.

A reminder for when you are negotiating a laundry machine lease. There are two ways to increase your share of the revenue. The vendor will try for a 60/40 split, but with just slight resistance you can get it up to 55/45, and with a little more persistence, possibly an indication that you wish to think it over and check the competition, you should get a 50/50 split.

At the risk of sounding cynical, I suggest that the second way is to put into the lease contract a clause stating that each party has a right to have a separate lock on the machines and that both parties must be present before they can be opened. Thus nobody will be tempted to skim some coins. Not everyone is dishonest, but don't project income greater than called for in my formula of $3 per month. There are exceptions to the $3 rule, but do not use them in your computations. For example, we have an eighteen-unit apartment complex, in which the laundry would normally be returning only $108 per month. However, our income has been running close to $185 per month, because there are no other machines on the entire block and the neighbors use ours during the day. If you followed the math you noticed I used $6 per month when my formula called for $3. This is because we own the machines and do not split with anyone. If the machines had not come with the building, I would be leasing, but they were already there and were made part of the deal.

SECURITY DEPOSITS

There are two types of deposits taken by the owner from the tenant, the nonrefundable deposit and the refundable deposit. Both are legal in most states; however, some states have outlawed the practice of nonrefundable deposits, making it mandatory to return the entire deposit if the residence is returned in an undamaged condition.

If your state does not allow a nonrefundable deposit, then do not record that income. However, if you are in one of the states that allows you to collect such a deposit, then assume each apartment will turn over once a year and count the nonrefundable deposit as additional income in your calculations.

VACANCY

Now that you have computed the gross income, the adjusted gross income is easily figured by subtracting an amount for vacancy and credit loss.

The column is named "vacancy and credit loss" because it covers not only empty apartments but also tenants who do not pay or who write bad checks.

Check with your seller and he will most likely tell you that his vacancy factor is generally zero. He will say that he always has a waiting list or that he rents the vacant units the first day he puts a sign out. I have even had sellers tell me they are running at 103 percent or 104 percent occupancy because tenants move out before the month is over and new tenants move in, allowing the landlords to collect double rent. But this is almost never the case. If what sellers tell you about vacancies were true, then there would be no "for rent" section in any of the daily or Sunday newspapers around the country.

I have been very successful using a vacancy rate of 5 percent or the seller's percentage if that is higher than 5 percent. I will never use less than 5 percent even if his books and records prove the number to be lower. I am concerned with the future and not the past. I must make an allowance for possible changes in the occupancy rate for the community. In 1979, Mesa, Arizona, had a 3 percent vacancy rate for apartments, but because of a changing economic climate the rate climbed to over 8 percent in only two years. Time can have a dramatic impact on vacancy rates. Before using 5 percent, however, check your community for its average. The local chamber of commerce, the property management departments of the banks, and the local board of realtors can help you arrive at a reasonable rate.

When you are dealing in a specialty type of building, do not use averages. You must be able to go over the seller's records for at least the last year. Naturally, two years' records would be better.

A typical example is a vacation apartment complex in Scottsdale, Arizona. The rent roll is $110,000 per year, but $80,000 of this comes during January, February, March, and April. Only $30,000 is collected during the remaining eight months. Furthermore, not only is the rent lower in the summer, but the building has a 60 percent vacancy rate. In June a prospective buyer would see a completely different picture than he would in January unless he had seen the books for the entire year.

Beware of the seller who counts the free apartment to the manager in the vacancy factor. A free apartment in a twenty-unit apartment complex eats up the entire 5 percent vacancy rate. Also, make sure any decrease in rent for the manager is included in the expenses (see below).

Expenses

Getting the correct income information can be tough, but trying to arrive at an accurate list of expenses can be *really* difficult. Most sellers will omit many of the expense items in hope that the buyer will overlook them. For each dollar a seller can hide, the value of his building can increase in excess of $10, so the incentive to hide is very strong.

The methods and formulas that I will give you to check expenses are not the only ones available, but they are the ones that work for me. You may come across simpler, more efficient methods, but make sure they are "seller-proof."

TAXES

Taxes are easy to check. Simply call the local authorities. Generally the tax assessor's office. The information is public record. If the seller gives you a tax bill, make the phone call anyway because the taxes may have been raised recently.

INSURANCE

Do not accept the figures from the seller even if he gives you the policy and the premium receipts. He may be correct in the current insurance amount, but that amount may be different for you, for these reasons:

1. The seller may be under a blanket policy which covers all his properties, and so his rate for the one you are buying appears lower.
2. He may be at the end of a three-year policy and the rates will increase considerably at expiration.
3. The amount of insurance he has may be less than the amount you need, since you are probably purchasing the property at a higher price than he paid.

The solution is to find an insurance agent, preferably a charter property and casualty underwriter (C.P.C.U.), who will work with you on your purchases. He will go out to the site and give you a quote on the amount of coverage you need.

Make sure he is aware of the fact that you are in the contemplating stage and that he may have to give you quotes on many buildings before you make a purchase. But also assure him that you will give him the business when you do purchase a building. Then follow through on your promise.

MAINTENANCE

Accountants break down maintenance into a number of different categories—pool, landscaping, repairs, remodeling, and so on. I do not look at maintenance strictly as a matter of upkeep. I also want to be sure I have allocated enough to cover unexpected problems.

In order to get a good idea of the seller's expenses for maintenance, ask to see his expenses for the past two years. This will also give you an insight into his method of management. His position will be one of two. If he says, "It's a good building, and it needs very little work," be very careful to check for "deferred maintenance" when you do the physical inspection. Deferred maintenance includes such items as carpet repair, painting, furniture replacement, clogged gutters, peeling paint, and missing vents. Bringing up these problems can be very advantageous to your side during negotiation. If the seller says, "I loved to put more into the building than was needed, so there is very little left for you to do," it is probably also a cover-up, but of a different nature. Depending on the age of the building, the seller is probably just trying to hide the normal maintenance expenses.

You can use a single formula to check on maintenance costs that don't seem to have increased over the years.

Give an "economic age" to the property and then apply the dollars necessary to maintain the building based on that age. For new buildings up to about three years old allow $10 per unit per month for maintenance. For buildings about four to fifteen or twenty years old I apply $15 per unit per month for maintenance. When the building is more than twenty years old I then allocate $20 per unit per month.

You have probably noticed I am rather loose with this timetable. If you are a parent you know all children do not go through their "phases" at the same age. I know some children who are adults at sixteen, while others are still teenagers at twenty-five. By the same token, buildings age differently too.

Property age should be measured by its *use,* not by a calendar. A student-oriented property can age very quickly if it is furnished and located next to a university or college. New property can look ten years old within three years. On the other hand, I have a condominium in Florida that is rented four months out of the year to a middle-aged couple from New York. The condo looks brand new, yet it is fourteen years old.

If you have doubt as to the economic age of a property, always select the older bracket and allocate the higher amount for maintenance.

SUPPLIES

This is an easy one where you can't go very wrong. I use $10 per unit per year to cover miscellaneous supplies, such as light bulbs, tape for the adding machine, rubber bands, and other such items.

PROFESSIONAL PROPERTY MANAGEMENT

If you hire a management firm to take care of your building, the cost can range from 3 percent of the adjusted gross monthly rent for a large building to up to 10 percent for a single-family home. Although you will probably manage the property yourself, it is best to add in such a fee. It is a valid expense, and it can be helpful in negotiating the purchase price. Also, a managerial fee might be figured in by a buyer when you sell the property in a few years (or months). There is also a possibility that you will move away and, wishing to retain the property, be forced to hire a professional management company.

ON-SITE MANAGEMENT

If you are purchasing more than one property, then you need an on-site manager. I realize that you may want the income and may be willing to do the manager's work to save the expense, but include this in your expenses anyway. When this is your only property, it may be easy to mow the lawn, clean a unit when the tenant moves out, show the unit to prospective renters, fix the toilets when they jam, or let a tenant in when he forgets his key in the middle of the night. But as you acquire more properties, these tasks become impossible unless you are available on a full-time basis. You will soon discover that your time can be better spent enjoying yourself or finding new properties to buy.

If you are the manager, you must remember to pay yourself for the work you do. A fair price for a manager is $10 per unit per month. This may sound low, but if you want to test it, put an ad in the Sunday paper for a manager at that wage and wait. Your phone will ring off the hook with eager prospects. If you keep a log of the hours you spend doing the work a manager would normally do (including traveling from property to property), you will find that you earn less than minimum wage, so you can see that it is not time well spent for you.

If you are hiring a manager, a married couple with a small child and one of the parents at home during the day is an ideal arrangement. They will be very happy for the added income, but I do not recommend you give your manager a reduction in rent. Pay him each month—the cash in his hand will be very motivating. He will appreciate his job more by getting paid monthly, whereas he may soon lose his appreciation for a reduction in rent. Furthermore, should you come across a buyer who uses the gross rent multiplier for his appraisals, you will have reduced your building's income by the amount of your manager's rent reduction, thereby costing yourself a great deal of money.

UTILITIES

I gave you some ideas of the problems associated with utility expenses in the first chapter. This is the one to watch; sellers love to get you here. If you can get a letter from the seller addressed to the power company allowing them to disclose the charges for the last twelve months, then you have a way to check. In lieu of a letter you can request to see twelve consecutive bills from the seller for each meter on the premises (unless the tenant is paying the bills for a meter).

When you check, pay special attention to the following:

1. Count the meters. A seller may forget to give you bills for each of them.
2. Check the year on the bills. Sellers have been known to "accidentally" give you a year in which the rates were lower.
3. Check to verify that the billing months are for consecutive months. Watch out for two January or February billings if you are in an area with high summer utility usage (i.e., air-conditioning), and for two June or July billings if you are in a cold-weather state.

ADVERTISING

I mentioned under the discussion of vacancy that there would be no need for the Sunday classified ads if every seller's building were 100 percent occupied. The truth is, you need to advertise, and the ads cost money. How much you will need to allocate for advertising is something you will have to learn from experience—there is no formula. You may need only to buy a large "for rent" sign (do not buy a cheap one), or you may have to run a one-inch daily ad in your local newspaper. Your location and your turnover ratio will determine your cost.

If the property is located on a well-traveled street you might get by with only a vacancy sign. However, if your property is buried on a side street without a "window" to traffic, you may have to explore other avenues of advertising.

REPLACEMENTS

Somewhere, somehow, you must take into consideration repairs and replacements that do not occur on a monthly or even yearly basis. Eventually you will be faced with major expenses, such as furniture replacement, roof repair, pool refinishing, and new water heaters. If you have not set aside money for these expenditures, you will be strapped.

I suggest that in your expenses you allow 3 percent of the adjusted gross income for replacement and repair.

MISCELLANEOUS

There are a few additional items to be included. They are small and may seem hardly worth mentioning, yet when added together they can make the difference between a building that produces a cash flow and a building that costs you money (a feed) every month.

Do not forget to figure a monthly cost for:

1. Legal fees. You may have to start an eviction.
2. Accounting fees. Who is going to do your year-end books?
3. Bank service fees. Banks do not process your transactions for nothing.

4. Deposits. Most utility companies require an up-front deposit or a bond before they will turn on power.
5. Licenses. You will probably need a sales tax license, pool license, boiler inspection license, and possibly even an apartment house license.
6. Other fees. If you plan to join the credit bureau, the chamber of commerce, better business bureau, or the apartment owners association in your community be sure to include these costs.

Check each item mentioned in this chapter. It's important. It is like checking your parachute before a jump or testing your oxygen tanks before an ocean dive. One oversight, one slip, one hole in your chute or leak in your tank and you are dead. If you make an economic slip you could be dead financially. If you pay too high a price because you did not check income or did not verify expenses, then you could be sitting on a property requiring a monthly payment out of your pocket. If you cannot afford the payment, you could lose the property and everything you have in it.

I have covered each item in detail because you will need all the information to deal with the seller during your negotiations. You based your original offer and terms on his figures, but now you have a more factual picture of the building and you will have to renegotiate. As you will remember, this was the reason for the "weasel clause." You will see in the later chapters how important the information in this chapter is for negotiating well.

CHAPTER

6

The Confrontation

Now you know the basics. We've discussed what you need to know about the contract, how to get the right realtor, and how to analyze your potential investment. You've been given the building blocks to work with, now let's see how you can make something out of them.

During real estate negotiations, buyer and seller meet face to face, where the facts are not black and white and where many outside influences control how far a buyer or seller will go. Armed with the knowledge from the previous chapters, we now venture into the land where a nervous twitch, a crack in the voice, a misplaced decimal point, or a careless reading of a lease can be a very costly error.

Set Your Limits

Before the actual confrontation, you need to establish your limits. By doing so, you set the absolute upper boundary on each item that you will negotiate, so that you will not be tempted to go further than you showed at the bargaining table.

Occasionally, I'll get a phone call from a desperate individual saying, "How do I get rid of this alligator?" or, "Can you help me sell this fourplex? It's eating me out of house and home." Almost always their problem is not the economy or the building, but terms of the contract. I usually discover that the owner paid more than he anticipated and if he is honest with himself, he knows he overpaid. Unfortunately, he fell in love with the property and used an anticipated rent increase or tax savings to justify in his mind the additional cost.

As you become a successful real estate entrepreneur you will learn not to succumb to such temptations. You will set your goals and stick to them. If you cannot purchase the property within your predetermined boundaries, you will have to go on to another venture. You won't try to make a deal fit or use the future to justify the present cost. You have to regard any future rent raises as a profit, not a means to cover too high a price.

To clarify this, let's suppose I purchased a building with rents of $1,500. After deducting for vacancy, expenses, and mortgage payments, I end up with a negative cash flow of $200. Even though I know I can raise the rent within the first two months to cover the negative, I would not be interested in the building, because the first rent raise would allow me only to break even and the building would not have increased in value beyond my purchase price even though I had increased the net operating income.

Also, do not be misguided when a seller says, "The rents are low; you can raise them as soon as you take over," or, "I know the tenants too well and can't raise the rents. However, you'll be able to." Face it: for whatever reason, if the rents were too low, the seller would already have raised them to get a better price.

Whenever you negotiate, establish your limits and base them on current figures, not anticipated increases.

Who Goes on the Presentation?

You know Pedro's story and hopefully you will not have a "Pedro" on your negotiating team. Whether you found the property for yourself or have used a real estate agent, the moment of truth is upon you. If you wrote the contract properly, and included a clause allowing you to accompany the agent, there won't be any problem. Although by law your agent has to let you accompany him, you also want him on your side. When you insisted initially that you would be part of all negotiations, he may have felt his professionalism and competency were being questioned, but you will have negotiated that arrangement so skillfully that he will feel you and he are an indispensable team of negotiators.

You may want to let your agent go alone to the first meeting. Most of the time he will not return with an acceptable counter-offer from the seller anyway, and you can then enforce your attendance at the next meeting. But even if the returned contract is only 5 percent less than the original listing price, you have won a major victory. When this occurs, you probably have an "E.T." situation where the seller wants to sell very badly. However, for our example, let's assume the worst. You have written an offer, your agent has delivered it to the seller's agent, who in turn has delivered it to the seller. It's now time to put yourself into the seller's shoes. He has received an offer far different from what his agent originally said the property was worth. He is disappointed and probably a little upset. His agent has inflated the value of the property in order to get the listing and now must defend his position; because your agent will not be present at that meeting, no one is there to present your side and most likely the seller's counter-offer will be close to the price originally listed.

At this point, a few kind words to your agent can set the stage for the next scene. A simple statement like, "We could go on like this for weeks. First, I would budge a little, then they would move a little, and we'd go back and forth until we either had a deal or walk away. Why don't we see if we can arrange a meeting with everyone needed to make a decision. This way we can negotiate all the items at once and get it over with. In a few hours we'll know if we have a deal or not and everyone will be happy. No wasted time or lost deals while we try to put this one together. Give their agent a call and see if tomorrow at 2 P.M. is good."

Get a Signed Counter-Offer

Whether you decide to meet with the seller or not, remember to insist on a signed counter-offer. If the agent comes with a verbal counter-offer, you have an agent who is not worth the commission he is earning and the time has definitely come to step in and take control. Under no circumstances should you ever write a second offer to a verbal counter-offer. It is worth the paper it is written on—nothing. Unless you have either a meeting with the seller or a written counter-offer, plan to walk away from the property and possibly from your agent as well.

Where Do You Meet?

If you are the one making the offer, you must convince the seller that you have what he wants—an offer. Ordinarily, the buyer calls, makes an appointment, and takes the offer to the seller. That is what the seller expects. But you are not ordinary. You are a super negotiator, and another cardinal rule of negotiation is *"do not conform to the expectations of others."* There are several options as to where you can meet; the seller's home or office are not desirable. Instead, pick the location best suited for you. Meeting in your home or your office can be arranged by saying, "Mr. Seller, this is Tony Hoffman. I have an offer on your fourplex and would like to meet with you to go over it. I'm sorry, this evening I have to stay home to watch my children and can't get out, but if you happen to be going out tonight and would like to come over, I'm at 44 N. 44th Street." It doesn't matter what excuse you give, the object is to get him away from his territory. The owner may show some signs of

indignation, but if you sound like a serious buyer, he will probably show up to look over your offer. Often the seller may
respond, "Well, Mr. Hoffman, why don't you just tell me what
sort of offer you have in mind?" Don't be persuaded to give
your offer over the phone. It will only weaken your negotiating
position and strengthen his. You see, having the "home advantage" in real estate transactions is similar to having it in a
sporting event: The oddsmaker will always give an edge to the
team or player with the home advantage. The "home team" has
the advantage of working in familiar surroundings and as a
result feels more confident and composed.

In much the same way, meeting with a seller at his home or
office gives him an edge that is sometimes unbreakable. When
he is at home in his comfortable easy chair, the need to sell is
not as pressing. He may have just finished dinner and is now
relaxing with the problems of the day behind him. Going to his
office can be even worse. There, he is the boss, the leader, the
decision-maker. He sets the rules when he establishes the time
for you to come to his office. He has the edge on you.

So the best way to present your offer is to reverse the roles.
Take the advantage. If you can't get the seller to your own
home or office, do the next best thing—get him to the property.
Sometimes, the site can be better for you than your house or
office. You see, he has a picture of his property in his mind. This
mental image is usually far better than the property actually is,
and should either of you discuss the property from afar, this
unrealistic picture will block the truth.

Meeting at the property site corrects this problem. It gives
you an opportunity to bring up the bad points of the building.
Try a few comments like: "It appears the roof has been repaired
recently. How bad was the leak?" "The lawn seems to have bare
spots. It looks like I will have to reseed this fall," or, "Look at
the gaps between the doors and the floors! The electric bills for
heating and cooling must be outrageous."

These are all questions aimed at weakening the seller, and putting dollars in your pocket.

Recently, I negotiated for an apartment complex in Hawaii at the site. The first thing I did after we seated ourselves in one of the units was to lean over the coffee table and fix one of the legs. When I straightened up, I apologized to the seller, stating, "I'm sorry, but I thought the coffee table might collapse under any pressure since the leg was twisted." I didn't have to fix it. In fact it would probably have withheld the weight of my briefcase and any writing we had to do, but when it came time to discuss the fact that all the units were furnished, I had an advantage—to be able to remind the seller about the quality of the furniture. Instead of hearing, "All the units are beautifully furnished," I heard, "All the units are furnished. Some furniture will have to be replaced, but most of it will hold up for a few more years." His position was totally changed. And so was mine.

Make Timing Work for You

Timing is just as important as location when it comes to getting the negotiations started.

The best ground rule for timing is to always be late. This may go against many of your ideals, but when negotiating, it's to your advantage to be delayed. You have something the other person wants. Tease him a little. Make him curious. Hold out and let the suspense mount.

The ideal waiting time is five to seven minutes. If you are later than that, the seller and his agent will start to get annoyed. When meeting at the property, your typical response can be "I'm sorry, an accident held me up," or, "I made a left turn when I should have turned right." Use any one of a multitude of other "excuses" for a short delay. Likewise, if the seller is coming to your home or office, be on the phone and ask him to be seated. Be sure he knows you'll be with him right away. That way he can pick up a magazine and try to become inconspicuous. It gives him a form of relief. But if you watch him, you'll see him skim the magazine three or four times, never reading an article. After a few minutes he will become a little more tense and less confident. Terminate your phone call now and begin the meeting.

Which Items Should Be Negotiated?

As I mentioned in chapter 2, every item is negotiable. Everything from the use of your name, to the date of acceptance, should be covered.

Each item you want discussed should be included in the offer-to-purchase contract with the anticipation that it is going to be negotiated or compromised.

Don't expect to have your contract accepted the first time out. If it is, you have either offered too much, made the terms too easy, or you are not asking for enough concessions. Don't make any of these mistakes. You want to be able to allow the seller to make changes in your original contract. If he feels he has gotten concessions, you will be more likely to get the deal you want. You should even put in a few items that you do not want, just to let the seller knock them out. You will put up an argument, of course, but you will finally concede. For each item he gets, for each little battle he wins, he is more likely to compromise on the items you really want.

For example, when buying a single-family home, I always include in the purchase contract an item or two of personal property I know I won't get. I have asked for baby-grand pianos, televisions, stereo systems, and in one case the entire household furnishings, linens, dishes, silverware, televisions, wall pictures, and even the lawnmower (I got everything but the silverware and two televisions).

Most likely, you can expect not to get an entire household, but asking for it makes getting the appliances (stove, refrigerator, washer, and dryer) easier. You can settle for "just those items." If all you have asked for are the appliances, you will probably get a counter-offer attaching a dollar amount to each appliance.

When negotiating the terms, if you only want to give $10,000 down, start at $5,000 or $2,000 down. If you want seven years on the financing then start at twelve years or ten years and work your way down. You won't get 10 percent interest if you ask for 10 percent. You need to start at 8 percent or 9 percent. Likewise, if you want to close in 90 days, ask for 120.

It amazes me how predictable buyers and sellers are! For some reason, in eight out of ten situations they will bargain to a middle position on everything. For example, suppose the seller asks for 14 percent interest and you start off at 10 percent; the chances are good that you will settle at 12 percent. Yet, if they ask 14 percent and you offer 12 percent the settlement point will be 13 percent. This concept applies to down payment, price, years, rate, closing time, leasebacks, guarantees, and every other item in the contract.

Let me give you a close look at a recent negotiation for a medical complex. A doctor who used 25 percent of the building was asking to sell the whole property for $590,000, with $180,000 as a down payment, and five years on the carryback note at 14 percent interest. A carryback note applies to the amount of equity the owner has that he is willing to let the purchaser owe him and pay at a later date. Naturally, the interest has to be paid during the time the money is owed. In effect, the owner is acting as banker.

After doing my homework I set my goals for a price of

$540,000 with $140,000 down, and 12 percent interest for seven years.

Meanwhile, the doctor also suggested in his listing he would lease back the entire building for one year and thereby guarantee all of the current tenants for one year. We were not concerned with the other tenants so much as we were concerned with losing the seller's tenancy after the one year. Our past track record showed that a seller moves out as soon as his lease runs out since he only agreed to stay to help the sale. To cover ourselves we wanted a four-year guarantee on his 25 percent of the building.

The chart below shows his original asking terms, our original offer, and the final settlement.

	Asking	Offer	Settlement	Comment
Price	$590,000	$490,000	$540,000	Exactly halfway
Down	$180,000	$100,000	$140,000	Exactly halfway
Term of Note	5 years	10 years	7 years	More to his side
Rate	14%	12%	10% 2 years 11% 2 years 12% 3 years	More than half our way
Leaseback	1 year	5 years entire bldg.	Entire building 1 year Seller's space 4 years	Exactly what we wanted

Remember, negotiate everything and *always ask for more than you expect, then settle for what you want.* In order to achieve your goal, structure your initial offer so it is reduced through negotiation to the level you desire. It will amaze you to see how many of the items settle exactly where you want them. The only way to get what you want is to ask for it.

Never Give In—Trade Off

Take a look at the following strategy conversation.

BUYER: "I'll offer 10 percent."
SELLER: "Fourteen percent is what I want."
BUYER: "Eleven percent is all that makes sense."
SELLER: "I'll come down to 13 percent, but it's the least I'll take."
BUYER: "Well, if I do raise the rents I probably can afford 12 percent."
SELLER: "O.K. you win, I'll give in to 12 percent."

Sound normal? It happens in every deal, whether it takes place in person or through a series of offers and counter-offers. Who really came out ahead in the above example? Since it ended in the middle, it may seem that both sides won. Twelve percent is probably what both buyer and seller wanted in the first place.

Yet, what appears as a victory is not necessarily so. The true winner here is the seller. He is the one who conceded to the buyer's offer of 12 percent. By doing this the seller has the psychological advantage of being able to collect on another issue more important to him. Had the buyer played his cards right he would have bartered in a different manner.

First he would have never let the other person give in. And second he would always place himself in the position of giving in, in exchange for another item. Compare the previous conversation with the one below:

BUYER: "I'll offer 10 percent."
SELLER: "Fourteen percent is what I want."
BUYER: "Eleven percent is all that makes sense."

SELLER: "I'll come down to 13 percent, but that's the least I'll take."

BUYER: "I can squeeze 11½ percent if I raise the rents."

SELLER: "Twelve percent—that's it."

BUYER: *"Okay you win. I'll pay 12 percent if you'll give in on the ten-year term of the note."*

SELLER: "I'll only go five years."

By changing the scenario around we have switched the advantage to the buyer. In this particular case the buyer gave in to the seller at the same 12 percent, yet in doing so he moved toward the next hurdle: the length of the note. The buyer made the seller believe he was conceding to 12 percent and requested a concession on a future item. Continuing the conversation:

BUYER: "Nine years and we can make a deal."

SELLER: "Six years. You can't expect me to leave my money in the deal forever."

BUYER: "If you make it eight years, we can settle it."

SELLER: "Seven years, take it or leave it."

BUYER: "Okay, I'll take seven years if you won't go further, but I want no interest payments for six months since I am conceding to your seven years."

SELLER: "That's crazy, I can see giving three months, but six months is out of the question."

BUYER: "Okay, I'll settle for three months, but you'll have to take $8,000 down instead of $10,000."

Beginning to see how it works? As the negotiation continued, the buyer received the seven years on the note he originally wanted but made the seller feel he had won both of the major battles. With this in mind the buyer was able to introduce a moritorium on the payments and interest, and get away with three months without the slightest argument from the seller. The seller felt happy not to have to give up six months. Three months seemed like a bargain after "winning" two previous major points.

But the buyer's "never give in, trade off" strategy didn't stop with the three-month moratorium agreement. He "gave in" to three months in a manner that would lead into negotiations of the down payment. As a professional, you will soon master the art of trading off. All it takes is a little practice.

Use Logic to Make a Deal

There will be times during negotiating with the seller when you can't resolve an issue. When this happens, simply use the facts. Logic is one weapon that will be invaluable to your negotiation arsenal. Use it. It allows you to approach the seller with the frame of mind necessary to reach a settlement based on facts.

Unfortunately, the seller is often not thinking logically. When he reads how real estate values have skyrocketed over the years, he naturally feels his property should be worth much more than it is. He may not be willing to admit that he paid too much for the property originally. When the banks are getting a premium interest on his loans, he feels he deserves a premium price.

When his real estate "friends" inflate the value of his property in order to get a listing agreement, the seller feels his own appraisal must have been right and that his selling price is reasonable. Sellers often talk themselves into a course of action without really looking at the facts.

As a negotiator your job will be to deflate those values, and you will do it with logic. Show the seller that the selling price does not make sense on the basis of the terms and building income. Have a list of recent sales in the area ready to show the seller. Let him see the actual transactions that have taken place in his neighborhood during the last six months or year. Go over

the income and expenses, the existing loans, and the proposed
notes in order to show him, on paper, how the property
becomes one that produces a negative cash flow, or "alligator,"
under his terms. Then demonstrate logically how your price
and terms make sense financially.

This method may not win him over initially, but you need to
make it clear that your purchase must make financial sense.
Allow him to sleep on what he has learned in your discussion.
You may be pleasantly surprised to see him come back with a
more realistic offer the next day.

Would He Make the Deal Himself?

If, during your early negotiations with the seller, he does not
agree with the logic of your offer, ask him if he would make the
deal he is asking for.

Most sellers want to believe they are giving an impression of
being open and honest. Leaving out some of the expenses, omit-
ting a vacancy factor, or boosting the rent roll, may seem to
them quite acceptable practices in making a deal. They don't
consider themselves dishonest. A particular seller may rational-
ize his leaving out maintenance or renovation expenses by telling himself that the new buyer will be doing maintenance differently. He doesn't bother to include a management fee (on or off
site) because "the buyer will probably manage the property
himself." He may have convinced himself the only reason the
rent roll is so low is that he has known the tenants for years and
he doesn't have the heart to raise the rents. Self-deception is the
biggest con of all.

When you run into one of these sellers simply ask him, "On
the basis of these numbers, would you buy this building yourself
under the same terms and conditions under which you are
willing to sell it?" When you get a witty owner who responds,
"I bought it once, didn't I," or, "I'm selling, not buying," or

some other equally evasive answer, come back with a very sincere, "If someone showed you a contract like the one I have here, would you accept these numbers, or would you substitute numbers you feel are more realistic in order to make a better evaluation of the building's worth?" By approaching the problem in such a manner you can do away with the seller's false presumption and get him thinking more realistically.

Of course you will have to be inoffensive in presenting your logic and yet still get the point across. If you offend the seller he will immediately take the defensive and become a real opponent. But if you make your point with feeling and diplomacy, you will be able to win him over and he will become more realistic and ready to make concessions. Remember, the key is your sincerity!

How Much Time to Allow for Acceptance

Let's say you have presented the offer to the seller in person and have gone over a few of the numbers with him. How long should you wait for his counter-offer?

Remember, one of the key elements of your contract negotiations is time. If utilized shrewdly, time can work for you, otherwise it can be turned completely against you. The ideal situation would be to write the following into the contract: "This offer to be accepted upon delivery or this offer is null and void." This clause usually applies only when you are buying a single-family home from people living in the house. But people selling anything larger than an owner-occupied single-family home need more time to think about a deal. Generally there are others to consult, a spouse or business partner.

In this case use a clause similar to this one: "This offer to be accepted within two days or this offer is null and void."

The seller will want as much time as possible. He can use the contract as a weapon to obtain a higher price. With an offer in hand he can call other agents and sellers and ask for a higher bid based on your offer. If he can get one, he will come back to you with the other offer and will attempt to start an auction. Don't allow this to happen. With an in-state seller, allow the two business days to accept or counter. If the offer is sent to an out-of-state seller, I allow only a week.

To avoid the "one against the other" tactic you need to do two things. First, *insist on a written counter-offer,* not a verbal agreement. Second, *inform the seller that you are looking at other properties* and if, at the end of the acceptance period, the contract has not been accepted, your offer is withdrawn, and you will make offers on the other buildings. It is imperative that the seller understand that you mean business.

I ran into a problem in this area just last year. As soon as my offer on a sixteen-unit complex was accepted, the seller stalled. I now felt he was using my contract as bait for a higher offer. My partner (unknown to the seller) called him and tried to purchase the building. The seller set an appointment with him for that afternoon and, as expected, used my contract as a wedge to get a better offer. An hour later, we decided to use his tactics to our advantage. My partner presented an offer for $7,000 higher than the offer he was holding. The seller said he needed time to think it over and within an hour called to inform me he had an offer several thousand dollars higher than mine and asked if I would like to beat it.

As planned, I courteously declined and withdrew my offer, stating that I was sorry we couldn't do business and that I had to go on to other properties. I made a point to leave the door open by requesting that, should anything happen with the other offer, he should contact me, and if nothing else had occurred in the meantime, we could possibly do business.

The next step was easy. My partner's offer was accepted. However, after review of the books and records, he executed his weasel clause and withdrew his offer unless the seller would lower his price by $15,000 ($8,000 below my original offer).

The seller balked of course and did not accept the new price and terms, so the contract expired. That evening he called to ask if I was still interested. I confirmed that I was, but added that I had offered on another property which would take much of my cash. Furthermore, I added that since my talking with him I had revalued his property and I would consider it only for $3,000 less than my last offer. Inasmuch as my offer was still better than his last one, he took it, and we turned his little ploy against him.

You can use time in your favor by allowing only a short acceptance period.

The Counter-Offer—Read It Carefully!

When you do get the counter-offer, read through the entire contract first. In this modern world of precision typewriters and high-speed computer printers it is very easy to duplicate a page or pages from a contract with just a few minor changes which can create a huge advantage for the other party.

It is not at all difficult to retype page 2 of a contract and substitute "buyer pays" in place of "seller pays" for items such as title insurance, closing costs, or escrow fees. Unless you reread the contract each time it comes back, subtle changes such as these will get right past you. I suggest you initial each page before it goes out and check for those initials each time it comes back. Do the initialing in a color other than black to distinguish a photocopy of your initials for the real thing.

Now that you've decided that the counter-offer is an original, read it very carefully. Remember, it is just the first attempt by the seller to test the water. He knows you are not going to accept his counter-offer and he wants to know in what areas you are most vulnerable. What he doesn't know is that you're doing the same thing. Look for what he is saying and also for what he is not saying. Try to read between the lines by asking yourself: Where has he moved most? Has he lowered the price, but kept the down payment the same? Has he given ground on the interest rate, but kept the due date on the balloon the same?

The movement in a counter-offer generally can tell you the seller's needs and wants. Figure out why he countered the way he did. His insistence on a down payment, for example, may mean he has a dollar obligation coming due. His failure to bend on the length of the carryback or wraparound (another method whereby the seller acts as banker by allowing the purchaser to pay only a part of the equity at closing) may indicate an obligation due in the future. Since you have set your goals, and are willing to walk away if they can't be reached, it is better to find out now if the deal is impossible.

Your agent's ability to find out the seller's motivation and limitations are very crucial at this point. If all your agent is doing is acting as a messenger for you, then the time has come to exercise your right to accompany him upon presentation. If he is doing his job properly he will get to the selling agent and find out which areas the seller is firm on and which areas are negotiable. Not all sellers are as smart as you and many of them will tell their agent which part of the counter-offer is soft. It's important, also, to bring up the points you consider critical to your decision.

Let your agent convey to the seller, in an informal way, that you are willing to negotiate on most items, but that if a particular item is non-negotiable and if it can't be resolved, then you will want to pass on the deal.

In Hawaii, the customary contract calls for only three- to five-year financing and many sellers will not budge. I have made many offers requesting ten-year financing and the counter-offers come back with three years. Through my agent I let the sellers know that my bottom line is seven years. If the seller won't concede to seven years, I pass on the deal. At the same time, I have accomplished another goal. By agreeing on the length of the note before our negotiations formally begin, I effectively remove this topic as leverage for a future concession from me. If I get an agreement before I write the new offer, the item is non-negotiable from that point and the seller cannot use it against me.

The 5 Percent Rule

When is a seller desperate to sell? On the other hand, when is he going to be hard to deal with? If you could answer these two questions you could reach your goal of financial independence very quickly.

I mentioned earlier that one guideline you could use is the 5 percent rule. If you make an offer, and the counter-offer comes back greater than 5 percent below the original price, you know you have an "E.T." and your chances of acquiring his property within your limits are very good. Suppose you were faced with this situation:

Asking price	$110,000
Your value	$ 99,000
Your goal	$ 90,000
Your first offer	$ 84,000
First counter-offer	$103,000

Your goal of $90,000 is very realistic because the first counter-offer was approximately 7 percent below the list price. It appears price will not be a problem and you can now look to solving other areas of the contract. Each time you make a new offer, increase your price just slightly until you are both equally distant from the goal of $90,000 and then suggest the two of you split the difference.

Your offer of $85,000 will probably receive an even $100,000 counter. (One tip: Sellers often make rounded counter-offers to rounded offers.) If the normal pattern continues, an offer of $86,000 will get a $97,000, and $87,000 will get a $95,000 counter. Eighty-eight thousand dollars could bring a $92,000 comeback, at which time you could suggest splitting the difference to $90,000.

Don't be afraid to move slowly with each new offer, since price will not be the only item negotiated each time. Because you use only written offers and counter-offers, the deal could take weeks to put together.

A Test of Nerves—He Who Cares the Least, Wins

This is a common-sense statement, but it is often lost sight of during the heat of battle.

All too often we forget that the seller wants to sell his property and we end up giving away too much to get it. It is very rare to see a buyer make an offer on a property that wasn't first offered for sale. The majority of completed contracts start with an owner offering his property for sale, either through an agent or by himself.

Remind yourself that he *wants* to sell and probably more than you want to buy. Then all you need to do is convince the seller of the same thing.

I teach a seminar on negotiations and at the height of the seminar is a workshop, pitting students against each other in one-on-one situations.

I give both sides the net operating income and the asking price and terms of the seller. Neither the buyer nor the seller is given any information about the opponent, but the seller is told he must sell and to get the best deal he can negotiate without letting the buyer get away. As I watch the students role-play, I can usually determine which seller will get the best price for his property. It is always the one who convinces the buyer he doesn't have to sell. But the moment the buyer gets the feeling the seller is desperate, he tightens the screws and gets a lower price and better terms.

In your own negotiations don't jump in with a new offer as soon as you receive the counter-offer. Be prepared. The agent will most likely ask you to write a counter that very same evening. Instead, wait a few days in order to demonstrate a lack of concern. By letting your agent convey to the seller's agent that you are also looking at one or two other properties, you will make the seller, and his agent, more than a little anxious.

In markets with more sellers than buyers, any buyer will be handled with care and agents will work very hard to get the seller to compromise his position in your favor.

Although there is the possibility you will occasionally run into a seller who will hold his ground for his price and terms, it is highly unlikely. As the buyer you have the upper hand, if you remember to use it.

A friend of mine actually opens negotiations, when dealing directly with the seller with, "I don't know why I am here. My wife will kill me if I buy another building like yours. I really shouldn't even make you an offer, but if the price and terms are right I may be able to convince her we should take on another property." He has immediately created the "he who cares the least, wins" attitude.

The Extra Edge—Eleventh-Hour Negotiations

The National Football League and the Players Union recently met at the Sheraton Hotel in New York City. It was late at night and a strike was scheduled for midnight if a settlement was not reached. Shortly before, a newscaster on the 11 P.M. television news stated, "After several months of meetings and attempts to settle the issues, the two sides are in eleventh-hour negotiations." What did he mean, and how does it apply to you and your real estate contracts?

When the end is in sight or something unfavorable could happen, such as a strike, the party with the most to lose will generally give in. It is up to you to persuade the seller that he has more to lose and then to demand a concession to complete the transaction.

As the purchaser you have a marked advantage because the majority of sellers have already mentally spent the money long before the actual closing takes place.

From the moment the seller signs the contract and accepts your offer he is planning on how to spend the money. In some cases it would be foolish for him to wait until he has the money in his hand before deciding what to do with it. Many times the seller will tie the property into a 1031 tax-deferred exchange to defer the taxes, or use the money as a nonrefundable earnest deposit on another house.

With this in mind, you can take advantage of the seller by just recognizing his vulnerability.

A day or two before closing, and even on the day of the closing, you have the power to demand and receive concessions, providing you don't go overboard.

What would you do as the seller if you had committed the proceeds of the sale and the buyer came to you to tell you he was going to be $2,000 short on cash and you would have to accept $8,000 instead of $10,000 down? Or if he came to you and refused to close unless the interest rate was lowered by one half point or, that he needed a moratorium on the carryback for six months until he could get the rents increased to cover the expenses?

Face it, if you stood to make a substantial profit on the sale, you would concede a minor item or a small loss. Who knows when you will find another qualified buyer? How long will it take to close a new deal? What will happen to the money you may have laid out for another deal if this one doesn't close? If you would concede, then you have to expect the seller to do the same. Take advantage of the situation; pick up a little extra on the deal.

Tell the seller he has to pay for the title policy and escrow fees or the discount points if there is a new loan. Tell him you didn't realize you would need extra cash to buy the impound account or to pay a large deposit to the utility companies. Let him know you have run out of dollars to spend.

Don't feel bad or upset about using eleventh-hour tactics to win a point. The seller would do it to you if he could. If he thought you had to buy the property he would try to get a little extra.

I used a classic example of this eleventh-hour tactic during the closing of an apartment complex a short while ago. All I did was refuse to close escrow until the seller would agree to subordinate his carryback to any new loan I might acquire to pay off the existing first mortgage.

His first reaction was total disbelief and a flat "no." But I knew that at closing the money was to be divided among feuding partners so there would be no problem.

The agent, after conferring with the partners, came back with a counter-offer requesting me to shorten the term of the note, in return for the subordination.

I stood my ground. I informed the agent I was not there to trade off. Either the subordination was included in the contract or there was no deal.

I gave all the money to the escrow officer and removed all contingencies subject only to the inclusion of the subordination clause. Then I left. Behind me was a dejected agent and a shocked escrow agent.

At 9 A.M. the next morning I received a call to come and close; everything was just as I requested.

Remember, you are in a war and you must use every weapon available to you to win.

We've covered a lot of ground in this chapter and it's worth pausing to recap the high points:

- Set limits on what price and terms you'll pay and then stick to them.
- Include in the contract a clause that states: "Buyer reserves right to accompany agent on any and all presentations to seller."
- Insist on a written, signed counter-offer; do not accept a verbal agreement.
- When meeting, avoid the seller's territory. Arrange to meet at your house, office, or, better yet, at the building.
- Never give in to a seller's request. Trade it off for another item.
- Use logic to convince the seller that your numbers are realistic, not his.
- If the seller still does not accept your analysis, ask him, "Would you make this deal yourself?"
- Read the counter-offer each time, checking all points for any changes made.
- He who cares the least, wins!!! If, after negotiating, the seller won't budge on an item critical to your goals, then walk away from the deal and go on to another one.

What to Do During the Contingency Period

Now the Countdown Begins

You may have thought negotiations were over when your offer was accepted by the seller. Not quite so. The true test of nerves begins now with the contingency period. This is the time when we find out what the seller is really made of. If you have written your contract correctly and included the weasel clause as I suggested in chapter 3, you should not have any problems verifying the seller's data before submitting your final offer.

Remember, all sellers are dishonest to some degree, so if you are not happy with your offer, you can always find something wrong with the income statement or the expense list that will allow you to walk away from the deal and go to another. However, you will never accomplish anything if you spend all your time writing offers and never completing a deal. The object of "catching" the seller in his "white lies" is to restructure the deal to make it a much more favorable proposition for yourself.

Of course, if you negotiated properly in the beginning you should have a pretty good contract already. Your price should be below market value (so you can sell it tomorrow at no loss if you need to). You should have good terms (low down payment and at least seven years on any balloon). And you should have a good interest rate (assumption and carryback). The seller is convinced he has fought gallantly for his position and has already spent the money. Just as this gave you the advantage in the eleventh-hour negotiations, it will also prove to be a psychological advantage during the contingency period. Greed has set in and the seller's profits are burning a hole in his pocket. Now is the time to strike.

Check the Seller's Information

Before you actually look at the seller's books and records, do a little undercover work. Assuming you are buying a fourplex or a larger building, dress in old clothes and take your dirty laundry over to the building after dinner or on Saturday morning. Put your clothes in the washing machine, take out a good book, and wait for another tenant to show up. Start a conversation with him and you will discover things about the building never before available to you. If the building does not have a laundry room you can accomplish the same thing by posing as a prospective renter and contacting the current residents personally. Tenants love to talk. You can find out about the heating, air-conditioning, water pressure, plumbing, and soundness of the roof. If you inquire further, you may discover some interesting facts about the vacancies, the noise level of the complex, management of the building, as well as the type of tenants presently living in the apartment complex. You must keep in mind that you are receiving a biased opinion from a tenant, but when this information is combined with the biased opinion of the seller, you should have a pretty clear picture of the actual situation.

With these new insights and your stockpile of formulas described in earlier chapters, you are ready to challenge the seller's information. Arrange a time to review his books and records. His information won't change your analysis too much since you will use your own set of formulas and guidelines. What you need at this stage is to make the seller aware of his vulnerability in order to give you a psychological edge in the negotiations.

How you handle this aspect of the contingency period will determine just how much more you can negotiate away from the seller down the road.

Do Your Work Out Loud

When the time does arrive to check the books, let me give you a tip: Do your thinking out loud in the presence of the seller. Too often buyers have the books and records delivered to them to examine at their leisure. Don't make the same mistake! You'll gain a greater advantage if you arrange to meet with the seller personally to go over the information. What happens if the seller claims he does not have time for you? Regard this as simply an excuse. Use pressure if you have to, but have him present at the inspection. To do this you may have to resort to verbal tactics such as, "I do hope you will be there to explain some of the information I will be looking at. Since I am new to income property investments, I may not understand it." Or better yet try, "If we discuss it at your office I can have access to all of the information at once instead of having to return each time I discover something else I need to examine." The fact is, sellers will gladly discuss their building with a potential buyer if your request is presented tactfully.

Once the inspection is underway, start weakening the seller's position. As you recall, you are trying to alter his mental image of the property. To do this, bring up each and every negative item you find and ask for an explanation.

During the recent negotiation of a twenty-one-unit apartment building I used this technique to get what I wanted from the deal. The seller and I had agreed upon a purchase price of $562,650 with $170,000 down. The offer included the assumption of the existing mortgages at 9½ percent and a carryback for seven years at 12 percent annual interest. By the time the contingency period ran its course the terms were $532,650,

$150,000 down, and 10 percent on the carryback with no payments or interest for the first six months. Comparing the two contracts, it's plain to see there is a considerable difference. The down payment was dropped $20,000 and the reduction in interest rate put $7,000 in my pocket the first year and $2,000 each year after that!

	Price	Down	Rate	Comments
Original agreement	$562,650	$170,000	12%	
Final agreement	$532,650	$150,000	10%	No payments

You may ask, how did I do it? First, I inspected the leases. I noticed that four of them would expire during the summer months (the time of my closing). Since Arizona is not a good rental market in the summer, I asked the seller to explain why he allowed four leases to end in July. After a good deal of hesitation, he confessed that the tenants really wanted to leave in May. Because they were in Phoenix only for the winter, three tenants actually did leave, forfeited their security deposit, and paid no rent for June. A closer look at his income statement revealed that this happened each year. Now that I had this information, I explained to the seller that we would have to agree on a more realistic total rent roll. I also gained agreement on the fact that rent would be slow in coming until January, the prime rental period.

The next step was to go over the utility bills and ask, "How much did the utilities increase over the last two years?" After he replied that it was 20 percent, I asked, "Do you think they will continue to increase over the next two years?" This question is always a good one to open with. Utility companies are noted for their annual increases, so this usually discounts the seller's statement. By hitting on each item, I was undermining his position. As a final blow, I approached him on the fact that he had neglected to allow for management expense. When questioned, he stated he did the management himself. I complimented him on doing such a good job and for having enough time to do it himself, and added, "I don't have the time to do it myself, so I will have to build in a management fee to hire someone to do all that work. Therefore, when I sell, any future buyer would also include a fee for management." The end result? The seller begrudgingly agreed that his net operating income did not justify the current terms and I was able to negotiate him down to the level agreed upon. The deal closed a short time later.

Physical Inspection: The *Piece de Resistance*

This is probably the most fun of all negotiations. The seller knows you are interested in his building, but realizes the whole deal can fall through if his building doesn't show well. He's nervous and you know it. It's like opening his home to you for inspection, hoping you won't find any skeletons in his closets or black sheep in his yard. Here, you definitely have the advantage.

When you do the actual inspection, make sure the owner is present. Inspecting with his agent or realtor will be somewhat helpful, but for the best results, you need the owner at the inspection. The realtor's presence is a bonus.

Here are four of the most important things you can do during the physical inspection that will make you an "expert":

1. *Never rush. Go through each unit slowly.* Check each room, turn on each light switch, check each appliance. Take pictures of all personal property. Turn on all water faucets simultaneously to check for a drop in the water pressure. Lift the top of the toilet tank and see the date stamped on the inside of the cover. If the lid hasn't been replaced, the stamped date will

reveal the date the building was constructed. Be very observant of the ceilings, especially in the closets. Water stains and discoloration could indicate a roof leak.

In the kitchen, look under the sink. Is the wood warped? This could be evidence of poor plumbing. What about the appliances? Do the burners on the stove work? Does the refrigerator run smoothly?

Once outside, check each storeroom and laundry room. See if there is any loose pipe lying around. Replaced pipe can show you how bad the water system is in the building. Either inspect the roof yourself or hire a professional to check it for you. Check the electrical system. Count the meters and then casually stroll over to the mailboxes to see how many empty nameplates there are.

Should you run into any tenants along the way, don't hesitate to ask them how long they have been living there and if they have any complaints about their unit. If they seem reluctant to volunteer this information, then ask leading questions such as, "How is the hot water when you take a shower or a bath?" Such questions will generally get them to talk. It's your job to make sure the seller can eavesdrop on their answers. By doing so, you bring the seller in closer touch with the problems in his building and weaken his position.

2. *Inspect all units.* If you are denied access to a particular office space or apartment, then that is the unit you want to inspect. I have heard more excuses for not being able to inspect a unit than I would dare to list. All are simply attempts to keep the purchaser from finding out the truth. Here are a few of my favorites:

a) "I can't go in without permission and they aren't home." This is perhaps the best-known delay mechanism. It just plain tells you to overlook this apartment and is tantamount to saying, "Go away and be a good little buyer." You must, of course, contend with such put-offs by refusing to accept them and by developing your own tactics for achieving what you set out to do. Whether this means returning later when the tenant is home or asking for written permission from the tenant to enter, do it! You must simply refuse to fall victim to such put-offs, no matter how many other buyers will play by these foolish rules.

b) "They have a baby sleeping. You don't expect me to wake him up, do you?" By putting you on the defensive and tapping your human emotions, the seller hopes to make you forget this unit and go on to the others. You can prevent this type of excuse from sabotoging your inspection by making it clear that you will be happy to talk briefly to the mother of the sleeping infant and arrange a time to inspect the unit at her convenience. Of course, if no one answers your soft but audible knock, you may decide to question whether there is current occupancy of the unit.

c) "I don't have time for all of them. Let me show you the worst ones." This typical delay device promises that you will be able to inspect the remaining units on another day, but of course, that day will never come if you don't pursue the issue. The ultimate goal of the seller is to keep you at bay and hope you will buy the building on the basis of the units you have seen. If the seller knows you will inspect all the units eventually, he may be just buying enough time to get the vacant units rented or repaired for your inspection. Whatever you do, don't let the seller put you off. If he doesn't have time to show you all the units, then maybe you don't have enough time to buy his building.

d) "The tenant changed the locks, and I don't have [or can't find] the key." This has to be the best ploy of all. With the first three excuses there is always someone else to blame, generally the tenant, but the "don't have the key" excuse makes the seller his own scapegoat. Remind the seller that a lost key or a locked door is not your concern. It is his responsibility to get the door open for your inspection.

An excuse, any excuse, should immediately raise a red flag.

Be alert and ready. If any unit is made unavailable to you, do not remove contingencies until you have made an inspection of that unit.

Steve Wallace suggested we look into buying a forty-unit apartment building that appeared to be a good deal. During the inspection the owner conveniently didn't have the key to open two units and a third unit "had a vicious dog inside."

Although there were minor items to be repaired, nothing Steve had seen in the other thirty-seven units would keep us from purchasing the building. Following the rules, he insisted on inspecting the remaining three units. A date was set for the following week and upon arrival, Steve entered the "vicious dog"-occupied unit. The carpet was torn to shreds, the drapes were sliced apart, and the furniture (property of the building), was torn and covered with dog hair. The smell was what you might expect from such an apartment.

Checking out the other two joining units proved to be much easier. The units appeared perfect. Too perfect. Each had been newly painted. Everything looked great.

Later that same day, Steve went back to the complex alone and knocked on the doors of each of the two units he had inspected earlier. Using the pretense of having left his notebook, Steve entered into a conversation with both tenants and was informed that the ceiling in both kitchens had collapsed from a bathroom leak in the apartment above, and to the best of their knowledge the problem had not been corrected. All the owner did was put up new drywall and repaint. According to the tenants, the ceiling would likely weaken and collapse again. A check of the seller's books revealed no payment for any repair of plumbing, so the tenants were correct in their assumption.

Knowing this, Steve recommended that we pass on the building because of not wanting to do business with the seller. We did.

3. *Take mysterious notes.* Throughout your inspection, carry a clipboard and a yellow note pad and take notes continually. Write down everything—good, bad, or indifferent, but keep writing. The more you write, the more nervous the seller will be. He will think you are writing down problems with the building. Remember, you are trying to devalue the building in his eyes.

4. *Voice your opinion.* Verbal comments were an important aspect when you reviewed the books and records. They also prove to be valuable during the physical inspection. As you stroll through each unit, let the seller know your impressions.

Each time you see something wrong, announce it to the seller as you write it down. Mention the crack in the ceiling or the kitchen tile that is twenty years old. Is there a leaky faucet or torn and worn carpet? What about any patches on the roof and the cracks in the driveway? Let the seller know you are aware of these problems and are not happy with them. Each little comment you make will unnerve the seller and increase your bargaining position as a seller.

The Cat Is Sick

Until now the seller probably felt he had a firm deal. The way you handle the letdown is critical. The tactics you use to break it to him that the deal is not going through as planned can mean the difference between writing a new contract and walking away from the deal empty-handed.

Consider the spinster lady who lived with her cat for twenty years, never taking a vacation for fear of leaving her feline companion behind.

At a local family gathering, her favorite nephew convinced her the cat would be safe and in good hands if she would only relax and enjoy herself on a well-deserved European vacation. Tragically, within two days after her departure, the cat ran in front of a car and was killed. The nephew, realizing the aunt would drop dead of a heart attack should she be told of the cat's demise, created an alternative plan.

The next day when the aunt called home from France she was told the cat spent the night out in the rain and caught a cold. From England, two days later, she was told the cat was taken to the veterinarian for shots to cure the very bad cough and congestion. From Italy, word arrived that her pet had been admitted to the animal hospital with pneumonia. From Greece, the message told her that the cat was failing. Finally, while in Switzerland, she was told the cat died and was given a beautiful funeral. The easing of the pain was essential to prevent shock and remorse.

During your negotiations, you must do the same. To immediately approach the seller with your entire list of building defects would be equivalent to telling the aunt her cat had died without warning. The seller will kill the deal.

To remedy this, you need to approach the seller strategically. Bring up the most obvious physical problem first and get an agreement. Then talk about the furniture you will need to replace. Once this is acknowledged you can use your revised version of the rent roll or the missing expenses to get the terms adjusted downward.

This strategy worked well in one of my negotiations. I was not only shocked to discover five vacancies after inspecting the books, but after waiting one month until the rainy season arrived, I was able to detect several leaks in the roof.

My disappointment in the rent roll was met with a "take it or leave it" reaction by the seller. Needless to say, I left it, knowing that he was angry because I wanted to change the deal. I tried to explain to him I wasn't changing anything. The new offer was based logically on the new numbers, and had the books proved the correct rent roll, I would have gone through with the deal. A week had passed when a call came from the seller's agent. He would stand by his rent roll projection and guarantee the rents for six months until the winter season. I thanked him and the next day I had a new contract. Step one was completed.

Shortly afterward, I apologized to the agent and explained I couldn't go through with the deal, because I had discovered the roof was faulty and I would need at least $7,000 to repair it, which I didn't have under the current terms. Had I known about the leaky roof I would have made an altogether different offer.

The agent was furious. You see, he had already made plans for his commission when his client had agreed to modify the contract. "Why didn't I tell him the first time?" asked the agent. "It wasn't necessary," I replied, "he had already called the deal off. How should I know he would come back with another offer?"

I suggested a six-month moratorium on the carryback in order to cover payments on the roof, if I could get a roofer to take six payments for his work. Reluctantly the offer was accepted. The "cat is sick" method broke the new terms to him in stages that buffered the impact of each demand.

Take Your Time but Keep Working

There is nothing wrong with being methodical in your checking process. In fact, I highly recommend that you take your time and check each item very carefully. Whether you are checking the books, the leases, the mortgages, the title, or even the property, do it slowly. This will give you time to verify the figures and put the seller on edge. He wants to sell his building and he will be nervous until the deal closes.

It is one thing to make him nervous. This is advantageous. It is another to make him angry. You can disagree without being disagreeable. If you appear to be stalling and not working toward removing contingencies, you will alienate him and find yourself dealing with a very stubborn seller, or with no deal at all.

The New Offer

When you are ready to make a new offer, plan to make all revisions to your offer in writing. Don't get on the phone with the seller or your agent and show your displeasure. That reveals your hand.

Do all of your checking and inspections, rework your analysis on the basis of the true numbers, write a new contract. Don't cross out or change the old offer. Although it is legal to do so, amending the old contract alerts the seller to the many concessions he is now giving up. Sure, he will probably lay them side by side and compare, but this way he will not be constantly reminded of the reductions each time he picks up the contract.

What to Expect From the Seller

What kind of response can you expect from the seller at this stage in the game? Anger and rejection. As he reads the offer, the seller is going to realize he's going to receive less than expected and he is rightfully going to be upset. However, don't let his anger get to you. If you end up dealing with an irrational person, don't try to compete with him. Whatever you do, don't try to get him to understand your logic immediately. Back off and let him calm down. This may take minutes, hours, even days. Take your time and let him think about it. The only thing you care about is getting your offer accepted.

It is your job, either by yourself or through your agent, to explain that you were prepared to go through with the original offer provided everything checked out. However, since then the situation has changed. Let him know that the new numbers do not match the original numbers and/or that you found physical problems with the building that you are not responsible for. Owing to these discoveries you were forced to make adjustments in the price, terms, etc. Then let him simmer and cool off. Don't try to force the sale. If anything, you should take the role of the hurt or injured party. Give the impression you had really counted on putting a deal together, and now the information is different. You have been lied to, deceived, and cheated, and now you want things set right. You want a firm deal, but you are willing to walk away if you don't get it.

Never Negotiate Against Yourself

If the seller does not react to your new offer, you must sit and wait. Do not make any other offers. You can have your agent check on the progress of your offer, but it must be clear to the seller that the call to check on the progress is the agent's idea, not yours.

The moment you show a weakness, the seller gains. However, if you don't negotiate against yourself by conceding points before he asks for them, he should come around to your way of thinking.

The Hidden Persuaders

If writing the contract was all there was to negotiating a deal, real estate investing would be a lot easier. You could simply find a piece of property you liked, submit an offer, and patiently wait for a counter-offer from the seller. But it's inevitable that human behavior comes into play. You see, there are two factors that are involved when you negotiate a real estate deal. The first, of course, involves the written contract. This is the basis of your half of the agreement. The other guy, however, has a totally different picture in mind.

And here is where the second factor crops up, the human factor. It is impossible to anticipate fully how the seller will respond to your offer or whether he will be willing to compromise. So it becomes necessary for you to read between the lines, to read your opponent, determine his needs, and take control without your opponent's knowing it.

You can't know how the seller will respond by simply reading his counter-offer. You will have to know how to "read" him as well. By recognizing which nonverbal messages are important you'll be able to know when the seller is submitting his "final offer," and when he will be willing to come to your terms. Learn to recognize his verbal negotiating techniques and the control is yours.

Body Language—Silent but Golden

Your body is constantly communicating, whether you know it or not. Some of the most meaningful messages are the unspoken ones. The tearful eye of a child, the proud smile on a new father's face, or a yawn during a business meeting says it all.

Recently, a friend of mine was interviewing a young man for a job, and after a few minutes with this potential employee, he stated that the position was filled. The young man's resume was ideal, but my friend knew from the beginning that the applicant would not do. His grooming was inappropriate for the job and his manner reflected a lack of genuine interest in the position.

In negotiating real estate you need to put your body language to work for you. The way you act and react during your negotiations conveys information about you to your counterpart. By knowing how to recognize the nonverbal signals of your opponent you can remain in control of the situation.

This is not an area to be taken lightly. Many people place more value on the silent messages they see than the words that accompany them. Think about it. If you were to tell anyone that you had a great time at a party after spending most of the evening quiet and away from the group, would they believe you?

Many times your body lies about you. Your quietness at a party may be translated as boredom when actually it meant that you were pondering a problem or contending with an upset stomach.

In all, how you interpret other people's body signals is up to you. I compare it to reading stock market reports. One expert will advise you to take a bullish position while another will tell you the opposite. The facts are the same, but the interpretations are different.

Many experts agree that a person sitting in a chair with his arms crossed is probably bored or trying to shut out the speaker. Yet he may be cold or just tired. I myself have never been convinced that a person who sits with his legs crossed at the ankles is more receptive than one who crosses his legs at the knees. However, you can learn a great deal by studying body language. But the ones that could help your negotiations are not the obvious ones found in the books on the topic.

For example, how many times have you heard the expression, "I want to look a person straight in the eyes"? The eyes can reveal what a person is really thinking. I have noticed that from about five feet or less I can tell when a person is lying because his pupils get smaller. I have witnessed this with my children, employees, tenants, and people I have negotiated with. Try it. But if you plan on telling untruths, do it outside in the bright sun so your pupils are small to begin with. No eye contact at all can, of course, mean that your adversary is unsure about the negotiation and may be hiding one of the items that I mentioned in an earlier chapter.

Being late to a negotiating appointment usually shows a certain lack of concern about the upcoming meeting. Being very late is irritating, however, and is usually interpreted as hostile.

A good negotiator takes advantage of the nonverbal habits of gestures, making them useful to his negotiations. Consider adding new behaviors to give you an edge over your opponent. As long as your body is going to communicate, why not train it to say what you want it to? Try the following ways to learn a language—body language.

EYE CONTACT

When presenting the offer to the seller, his secretary, or anyone else, look the person in the eye. This will give the impression that you are confident about your offer, know what you are talking about, and mean business. Avoid drifting away in thought while negotiating. Keep alert and pay attention. When you want to communicate agreement, nod your head, and when it's appropriate, shift or tilt your head to reveal doubt and apprehension.

HAND AND BODY SIGNALS

Stand tall and sit straight so you look responsible, strong, and alert. Keep your hands poised to appear calm and composed. I notice as people get more nervous, they begin to fidget with their hands. You will seem to have more control over your emotions and the situation if you don't give yourself away by your gestures.

Body language plays an important role in negotiations, but there are no steadfast rules, only guidelines. Watch your opponent, watch his moves and reactions. Pay attention to his movements as he reads the contract and responds to the different paragraphs. He may glance at his realtor, his wife, or even at you when he reaches a particular clause. Make a mental note; these clauses will generally be the areas of major disagreement. Unless he is a professional and can hold a poker face he will reveal what he is really thinking.

Remember, the more you understand the other guy, the easier it is to make a deal. The reverse holds true for you. If he tries to "read" you, be on your toes. Don't give away any information about yourself through unintentional body language.

DRESS

Whenever I go to an appointment with a potential client I wear a suit. To negotiate with a tenant I wear something more casual. How you dress is important to the message you wish to communicate. If you want to be viewed as a professional then dress like one.

Dealing With Different Cultures

If you have ever been to Tijuana or Juarez, Mexico, you are aware that haggling with the merchant is the accepted way to do business. It is not unusual to get an Indian rug priced at $150.00 for $50.00 after a heavy and possibly lengthy bargaining session. And most likely the fellow behind you will get the same blanket for $75.00. It is all part of the color and culture of Mexico. To do the same in the States would be viewed as rude or insulting.

In real estate it is common to see different approaches to making deals with members of different cultures. What is acceptable to one ethnic group would be offensive to another. Some people do not want to pay full price for anything and expect intricate negotiations from you as well. Others will set prices and stick to them—even when they are unreasonable. You will have little or no room to negotiate so you have to approach these shrewd businessmen from a different angle. But if your offer isn't at their price and on their terms, they will probably refuse it and wait for someone else to come along.

With some people, a deal is best preceded by an informal drink or dinner. To rush into signing a contract would be viewed as rude and unprofessional.

In some areas of the country, a deal can't even be made until the person you are negotiating with is sure you know what you're doing. And I have found that, strange as it may seem, the more formal an education a person has, the more verbal foreplay is necessary prior to negotiating a deal.

Therefore, you should be aware of business and family norms in the community where you plan to buy. Sometimes it is viewed as essential to discuss the real estate deal in the presence of a spouse, yet to many, such actions would be interpreted as offensive.

It is not a good idea to generalize about any one culture. To broaden your negotiating ability you must be able to adapt to the differences each culture has to offer. The "touch" for dealing with various groups of people will come only with experience. Soon you will know what it will take to close a deal. You may want to keep a journal. Before long you'll notice a significant trend and be able to use it in your negotiations.

Attacking the Zone

Have you ever had anyone invade your space? Consider these situations.

1. You are in a theater and for the first hour no one uses the armrest between you and the person in the next seat. All of a sudden you feel his elbow on the armrest. You don't have to see it, you know it's there. Suddenly, your elbow is itching to use the armrest. You can't wait for him to reach for his popcorn so you can take over the armrest.

2. You are at a party chatting with a group of friends when a good-looking member of the opposite sex approaches to stand right next to you. Don't you start to feel nervous, wondering whether your hair is in place, your breath okay?

3. You enter a crowded elevator. Everyone is facing forward looking at the floor indicator. No one dares to talk or glance at anyone else. When everyone gets off except you and another person, watch him; he'll immediately move to the opposite side of the elevator to increase his space. Try walking into a crowded elevator and stand facing the crowd. Don't turn around, look at the other people. No one will look back at you. They will do everything they can to avoid eye contact.

It is well known that we regard the space around us as a very personal zone. It is only a distance of about arm's length, but we protect it. The moment someone enters this space, he or she is too close for comfort.

Knowing this can be invaluable to your negotiations. A comfortable person is a comfortable negotiator. Make him nervous and his mind will be occupied with your actions, not what is in the contract. Then you have the advantage. One simple way to do this is to discuss the contract while sitting beside him or her, not across a desk or table. Your opponent's space will have been invaded and his comfort destroyed.

Don't Let Them Get the Best of You

You may recall that the last place you want to make your offer is in the other party's office. Unfortunately, in spite of everything else, you may end up there. In that case try a few of these techniques to avert any tactics he may try.

1. *You arrive and he is not ready to see you.* This common ploy is used to keep you waiting and make you anxious. Set your own time limit. I will not wait more than seven minutes. If after a few minutes you feel you have waited long enough, leave your card with the secretary and either state you will return at a more convenient time or ask for her boss to call you for a new, mutually convenient appointment. Then walk out.

Sometimes you may really want to speak with the individual, in which case you are willing to wait in his office longer. If this is the case, then instead of reading one of his magazines, pull out a report from your briefcase and start to work on it. When he finally comes out of his office, apologize and let him know you will "be right with him" just as soon as you finish your thought.

2. *You are greeted and given a tour of his office.* This is a surefire way for your opponent to show off his power. He'll probably be very friendly, casual, and perhaps even go so far as to introduce you to his employees. These people, of course, all play

homage to this power play. Your best bet is to avoid any tours, refuse courteously, and promise to see his office when your time isn't as limited.

3. *Once inside his office he directs you to sit down and then makes a "quick" phone call.* This is a common power play. The only place he will have for you to sit in his office will be chairs well outside his zone. To counter this tactic tell him you prefer to write on a hard surface and pull the chair up beside his desk. If he has gone through the trouble to make sure the chairs in his office are all lower than his, then try standing up and saying, "You don't mind if I stand do you? I've been sitting all day and my back is acting up." Now you can lean over his desk and hand him the contract. You have taken the advantage.

Power Phrases

Hardly anyone has survived the childhood years without hearing phrases like,
"Sit down right away!"
"Clean your room like a good child."
"You better not do that again."
Sound familiar? Our parents intimidated us into doing various things by using common phrases which had a lot of authority associated with them.

As an adult, you may still carry leftover habits from your childhood which make you very vulnerable to authoritative statements which I will call "power phrases."

Power phrases are words used by those who wish to take control of the situation by putting down the individual they are with and then building authority for themselves. Professionals and authority figures are renowned for using power words to get what they want. Doctors, lawyers, professors, executives, politicians, etc., exert power phrases on a daily basis. Simply by expecting to be addressed by their titles, such as "doctor," "professor," or "sir," these people are able to exercise power over you. Below are some power phrases commonly employed to establish authority and control of real estate negotiations.

1. *You should know that* . . . This clever little device is usually accompanied by something like "the buildings in this area are selling for $30,000 per unit," or, "this price is well within market price," and are designed to engender doubt in your mind about your own knowledge of real estate. This technique implies that you should know these facts or that you would not question the statements being made. Don't be conned into not asking questions simply because you are afraid someone may think you do not know the answers. Reply to these power phrases with "No, I don't know. According to my statistics your building is only worth $25,000 per unit." Such a straight-from-the-shoulder approach must be used to prevent future "you should know" phrases. Once you try it a few times you will find it easier to confront these individuals and they will cease to use this futile phrase on you. Similar phrases are "it should be obvious" and "you can see that."

2. *If only you had* . . . It may be true that if only you had bought the building three years ago, you would be a lot richer. The best response to an "if only you had" power phrase is, "You may be right, but we could talk all day about what I could have done and that would get me nowhere." Or better yet, "If you can get me a round-trip ticket back to that time and place, I'm ready." Or, "I am more concerned with what I can do today. What can you suggest for that?" This returns the advantage to you. When in doubt about any power phrase being imposed on you, use logic to battle it. You will show your adversary that you are wise to his game.

3. *You did mail the check, didn't you?* Here is a phrase professionals always use. It can also take the form of "You did sign the contract, didn't you?" or "You did bring the papers, didn't you?" This ploy is a way of turning a simple question into a test, giving the questioner the upper hand and placing the recipient in a defensive position. Don't be intimidated by this method. Respond with "Yes, I did (or no I didn't), I told you I would (or wouldn't)."

4. *Of course not* . . . This power phrase is used to respond to a statement that may threaten the authority of the power figure. "Record the deed? Of course not." Or, "Did I inspect the building? Of course not." Be aware of such phrases. They are a way of covering up a mistake or something he overlooked and should have done.

You will know by now that strength is the name of the game in negotiating real estate. People respect those who deal from strength. When exposed to power phrases during your negotiations, recognize them for what they are: attempts to manipulate you into an inferior position. Avoid falling into such a trap. Think and respond logically. At first you may have to take your time to make an appropriate response. Logic has no ego and cannot be countered by intimidation.

And as you gain your confidence, teach yourself techniques that will help you operate from strength and confidence. When in doubt about a property don't ask, "Would you mind if I ask about . . ." Instead state, "I'd like to know about this. . . ." Replace "Do you think $80,000 is enough for an offer?" with "I am going to offer $80,000. When can I expect a response in writing from the seller?"

Work on your own verbal messages, particularly toward eliminating the "hmms" and "you knows." These verbal habits signify doubt and ignorance. If possible, teach yourself to talk deliberately and concisely. With a little effort your weak language can be switched to a high-power tool that will help you to negotiate.

The Double Power Play

Who wins if you're both playing a power game? You do if you are willing to pursue your advantage. I have had people come to my office and laugh when they see my chair higher than theirs and tell me, "That trick won't work, I know what you're up to!" I compliment them on their alertness and tell them they are right, but it was worth a try. What they don't know is that even though they are aware of it, they didn't do anything to correct my advantage. I still have it. Their inferior position remains inferior.

A short while ago, I was negotiating with a seller in his office when I noticed that my chair was in fact, lower than his. To counter his power I casually pulled my chair around to the back of his desk so I was sitting directly to his left. I leaned toward him with my entire body while I touched the contract to highlight a point. Needless to say, he pulled to the right unconsciously and as he did, so did I. He was so nervous he moved to the right of the desk and I was centered over the contract. I had resumed control within two minutes.

Use your knowledge effectively while negotiating. Exert your know-how and don't be swayed by verbal or nonverbal power plays. In the end the control will be yours and you will achieve your goals.

Four Steps to Getting Your Own Way!

Life can be complicated or life can be simple. The decision is up to you. You can learn the four steps to getting your way or you can continue through life, having to battle each point and finding yourself on the winning side less than your share of the time.

Think how few arguments you'd have had if you had been able to get the other party to see things your way.

Naturally, your way is always the right way, and the ideal solution to all problems is to get the opposition to suggest that things be done your way. Then you can agree and have your way without any disagreement.

There are four basic steps to any objection you are given and if you follow these steps you are on your way to becoming a master negotiator.

STEP 1: AGREE AND REPEAT

Example: "I can certainly understand how you feel, you would like 30 percent down on the sale of your house."

STEP 2: ANSWER

The next step is to answer the objection in the best way you can.

"I would also like 30 percent down if I were selling my house. However, in today's market 30 percent down would not be a good investment for me, when there are so many other sellers who would take less down. Just what would you use all that cash for? Did you know that if you didn't take the cash you could . . ."

STEP 3: ASK A CLOSING QUESTION

Nothing happens until you ask for the sale. Following our example: "Did you know that if you didn't take the cash you could be guaranteed 26 percent annual return on your equity each year with a seven-year note?"

"Now would you like a seven-year guarantee or would you

prefer to leave your equity working at 26 percent for ten years?"

The way you ask a closing question will determine your success. Each question must be asked in such a manner that either answer is a winner for you. Always word each question carefully, allowing answers that only come out positive for you.

STEP FOUR: SHUT UP!

This is the most important step in the entire list. Once you have asked a closing question, you are committing suicide if you open your mouth. Anything you say after asking a closing question relieves the other party of the pressure you have placed on him. When you are able to sit back quietly, waiting for a response, no matter how long it takes, you give the other party three choices: to go along with choice 1, to go along with choice 2, or to give you an objection. If he elects one or two, you win, if he comes up with another objection, you just go back to step 1 and start over. Eventually, you will end up with your way or you will be able to isolate and find out the real reason. The rest is a cakewalk.

Remember, even a fish wouldn't get hooked if he kept his mouth shut!

Get the Facts on the Contract

Financing is one of the most critical points of your negotiation. Naturally price is important, as is the amount of the down payment. However, the key to creating a deal that will work best for you will depend on your ability to negotiate good terms on the financing, and then stipulate them in the contract.

With today's high interest rates, it is practically impossible to finance a purchase with a new bank loan and still have it make good financial sense. It is not totally impossible, but it is very difficult. So it will be up to you to utilize what real estate investors have found to be the best alternative to institutional loans: seller financing.

Although it may seem odd, you should consider the seller as the first source of financing for your deal, primarily because he is in an excellent position to carry back a second loan for the equity he has in the property. But also, the seller is often able to "wrap" his existing loans with an attractive deal on a first mortgage. In a wraparound contract the seller retains his current loans and collects from you at a higher rate than he is paying. You will find an example of a wraparound loan later in this chapter, on page 134.

What type of seller financing should you negotiate with the seller for? In general it will depend on how much he is motivated, or wants to sell the property. An E.T. will obviously work to negotiate good terms, knowing that you will walk away from the deal if you can not agree on the financing. Under those circumstances you will be able to call most of the shots. However, before you decide which type of seller financing you want, you will have to consider carefully your position in the deal, or which side of the table you are negotiating from. If you are the buyer, the terms will be different than if you are the seller.

The Buyer's Choice—Assumption and Seller Carryback

As the buyer you want to assume the seller's existing loans so that you'll also be able to assume his lower interest rates. Obviously, if he has an 8 percent loan, it is to your advantage to assume it. Many banks and savings and loan institutions will try to prevent the assumption of a low-rate loan, but stick to your guns. Assuming a seller's existing loans could mean the difference between having a building with a positive cash flow and having a cash-eating alligator.

In addition to assuming the seller's existing notes, you will give the seller a carryback note for the amount of equity he is leaving in the deal. For example, let's say that you decide to buy a fourplex from Mrs. Nichols for $100,000. You put $10,000 down and Mrs. Nichols agrees to let you assume the $60,000 loan that now exists on her fourplex. This leaves $30,000 in equity to be financed. Since she is anxious to sell her building, she agrees to negotiate to carryback a second mortgage (or trust deed) as security for the $30,000 you owe. You sign a promissory note agreeing to repay the $30,000 plus interest over a specific time period. And you have made a deal.

In the body of the purchase contract then, you should include a clause that reads:

> Purchase price to be $100,000. Purchaser to give seller a total of $10,000 at close of escrow including any earnest money deposit, leaving a balance of $90,000. Purchaser

agrees to assume existing loan of $60,000 under the same terms and conditions of said loan. Seller agrees to accept a note for $30,000 secured by a mortgage (or trust deed), payable monthly, interest only at 10 percent per annum with entire balance due seven (7) years from close of escrow.

I specifically stated seven years, not three, five, or six. Seven years is the key to making sure you don't get in trouble with short-term notes and possible foreclosure. Aside from this, there are two reasons for choosing seven years as the minimum.

The first is that during any seven-year period in the economic history of the United States there has always been a good time to refinance a loan whose terms were less than favorable. This is not true with shorter notes.

Think back to the early and mid 1970s, when people were buying property with short-term notes of three years or less. At that time the short-term financing presented no problem since property was going up 25 to 30 percent per year. Three years later people went down to the bank and obtained a new loan on the current value of the property, paid off the seller, and owned an investment with a new long-term first mortgage and a large equity.

But at the end of the 1970s and during the first two years of the 1980s everything changed. Property values didn't go up, but the interest rates did and suddenly people couldn't run down to the local bank and get new financing. What happened instead were too many missed payments and subsequent foreclosures. If these people had had seven-year notes instead of three-year notes they could have kept up their payments until late 1982 or early 1983 when the rates came down and financing again became available.

The era of the "greater fool theory" was over. No longer could people buy property at any price knowing that a "greater fool" would come along and buy it from them at a higher price. Buyers and sellers became more sophisticated.

Secondly, if you have a seven-year note when you purchase, then two years later, when you are ready to sell the property, you will still have five years remaining, and there will be many people who will be happy to take over a five-year note.

Of course, this financing clause can be expanded to include more than it does in this chapter, but it does cover all of the principles we have discussed so far, and can be modified as necessary if the seller will not agree to all of these terms. However, you must be willing to walk away if the terms do not make good financial sense to you.

Seller's Choice—the Wraparound

What is good for the buyer is not necessarily good for the seller. When the time comes to sell your property, the wraparound should be the vehicle you negotiate for. As a seller you need to negotiate from a different perspective and this method of financing suits the seller much better than the buyer.

Let me explain why. The wraparound, also known as the "all-inclusive trust deed or mortgage," is a loan that is subordinate to, but includes all of, the existing loans it covers. It is a junior loan created by the buyer in favor of the seller to cover the unpaid balance of all the existing loans on the property, as well as any future encumbrances that may be placed on the property by the seller. This allows the seller to remain responsible for the existing mortgage while giving him the opportunity to make added interest or "spread" on the equity he holds.

To illustrate, let us suppose Mrs. Nichols received an offer to purchase her fourplex from Mr. Smith, who agrees to buy it for $100,000 with $10,000 down. That leaves $90,000 to be financed. Now, Mrs. Nichols is currently paying on a twenty-year note at 8½ percent with a remaining balance of $60,000. During negotiations, Mrs. Nichols convinces Mr. Smith that the only way she will sell is to take a wraparound note for her 8½ percent note. Mr. Smith agrees, and creates a promissory note for $90,000 with interest at 10 percent per annum. In the purchase contract (or in Mrs. Nichols's counter-offer) she includes a clause that reads:

> Purchase price to be $100,000. Purchaser to give seller a total of $10,000 at close of escrow including any earnest money deposit, leaving a balance of $90,000. The $90,000 shall be paid in the form of a note, secured by a deed of trust (or mortgage), payable monthly at 10 percent per annum, interest only, with the entire balance due seven (7) years from close of escrow.

Look what has happened. First of all, on her $60,000 existing mortgage that will be wrapped, Mrs. Nichols will receive $6,000 per year (10 percent of $60,000). But she will only pay out an annual interest amount of $5,100 (8½ percent of $60,000). In essence, she will make an extra $900 on the deal by charging the buyer more for the note than she is paying out.

Furthermore, since Mrs. Nichols will receive a total annual interest of $9,000 (10 percent of $90,000) and pay out only $5,100 on the underlying mortgage, her net will be approximately $3,900 a year, which is equivalent to a 13 percent annual return on her equity ($3,900 divided by $30,000 equity = 13 percent). In the meantime, she can continue to deduct the interest she is paying on the underlying loan from her taxes.

The following table will help clarify the different advantages to you as buyer and seller.

As the buyer:

Sales price $100,000

	A (assumption/carryback)	B (wraparound)
Mortgage	$60,000 × 8.5% = $5,100	$90,000 × 10% = $9,000
Carryback	$30,000 × 10% = $3,000	—0—
Total interest paid	$8,100	$9,000
Total Loan Amount	$90,000	$90,000
Buyer's Effective Rate	9%	10%

The buyer saves $900 and 1 percent by using plan "A," the assumption and carryback (does not include assumption fees).

As the seller:

Sales price $100,000

	C (using wraparound)
Seller collects	$9,000
Seller pays	$5,100
Seller's yearly profit	$3,900

The seller's return on equity is 13 percent ($3,900 divided by $30,000 equity = 13 percent). Therefore, under plan "A," the seller makes 10 percent on his money by taking a carryback, yet under the wraparound plan "C" he makes 13 percent because of the extra $900 he makes every year on his existing $60,000 note and the $3,000 he earns on his equity.

How to Convince the Seller to Carryback

In your purchase negotiations with the seller you might bring up some of these points:

1. The seller has the right to foreclose if the buyer does not keep his payments current.
2. You will walk away from the deal if the seller cannot arrange reasonable financing that fits your needs.
3. The seller can sell the second trust deed or mortgage for instant cash and take the discount as a tax write-off.
4. The seller's income will be steady and he will not have to be responsible for existing loans.
5. The seller can get a better price if he holds an assumable low-interest note.
6. This method makes his property more attractive to buyers.
7. He will earn an interest rate better than what a bank savings account would pay.

How to Convince the Buyer to Create a Wraparound

As a seller, you will want to convince the buyer of your property that he will benefit if he accepts your terms for a wraparound loan. Here are some points that you may want to include in your negotiations:

1. A wraparound requires a lower down payment, which creates better leverage for the buyer.
2. It's easier to qualify for the existing loan than if you had to apply for a new loan.

3. It saves costs on new loan appraisal fees, points, prepayment penalties, etc.
4. You as seller will tailor the payments to fit the buyer's ability to pay.
5. It saves time in shopping for a new loan.
6. It eliminates any assumption fees.
7. The buyer makes only one payment a month, not several.
8. Greater leverage means a better tax shelter and use of dollars.

Third-Party Clause

Whether you are involved in a carryback/assumption or a wraparound, you will need a neutral third party to act as a collection agency so that all parties are protected. In many states, collection departments are established specifically for the purpose of collecting funds from buyers and distributing them monthly to the appropriate recipients. In other states, banks or savings and loans perform this service.

To ensure that the payments you make are applied toward the loan you signed, be sure to include a clause in your contract to purchase that states the following:

> Third party (name of collection agency) is instructed to pay all underlying encumbrances first, and the balance, if any, is to be paid to the seller.

This accomplishes two things. First, it forces the collection agency to protect everyone's interest. Second, it prevents you from waking up one morning only to find that the payments you had made to the seller never made it to the bank and that foreclosure actions are being taken. The following story will show you how important it is to include the third-party clause.

A Valuable Lesson

In 1974, I purchased two single-family homes from a very prominent realtor and made the payments directly to him.

After doing repairs and improvements I attempted to sell the properties. The prospective buyer wanted title insurance so I ordered a preliminary title report. Needless to say, I was shocked when I discovered that the buildings were in foreclosure. Within the next thirty days, the bank would own the properties and I would be out.

What had happened? The realtor was getting my check on a regular basis, but not forwarding his payments to the bank. Fortunately, I learned about the problem while there was still time to do something about it. I called the realtor and made it quite clear that his reputation was at stake. He quickly obtained a new loan which would be assumed by my buyer and everything turned out for the better, but it could have been a disaster.

Convenience is another reason for the third-party clause. The third party will hold the deed to the property and will turn the deed over to the purchaser upon the payoff of the debt. Assume for a moment that in five years you want to pay off your note. You send the balance to the collection agency, and having fulfilled the obligation, you are entitled to the deed. What if the seller has moved and can't be located? What if the sellers have since divorced and they are not talking to each other? Or even worse, what if the seller has died?

Legally, you are not affected. You are entitled to a title and will receive it, but it could take years in court and at great expense. Meanwhile your property cannot be sold because it's tied up! All of this can be avoided with a little foresight when closing the deal by including the third-party clause. Cover all your bases—always!

What Is a Fair Interest Rate?

Before we discuss the other financing points that may be included in your contract, let us look briefly at interest rates. What is a fair rate of interest you can expect to pay?

If you believe what you hear and read, then you probably expect to pay between 12 and 20 percent for a second mortgage or trust deed. This is what banks and savings and loans will tell you.

However, there are many sellers who will make loans to you at 11, 10, or 8 percent and even with *no interest.* In 1983 I made a deal for $160,000 at 10 percent, and one before that at 8 percent.

If you are willing to give the seller a fair price, he will be willing to work with you on the interest rate. Do not be afraid to ask for a low interest rate. You might even ask for a moratorium on all interest, in which you make no payments for a specific period of time. I did this on two different purchases, and in both cases, it worked.

The first was a single-family home I purchased for $130,000 with $5,000 down and no interest or payments for one year. That is equivalent to 0 percent interest for the first year.

On a second purchase I negotiated for a one-year moratorium but the seller refused. We finally settled on a moratorium on all payments for the first six months and then an *annual* rate of 10 percent for the next six months. That is an effective annual rate of 5 percent for the first year.

If the seller tells you, "The banks are getting 17 percent; I want at least 15 percent," you can counter in several ways. One reply is, "You're not a bank Mr. Seller. If I wanted to pay those rates I'd go to a bank!" Your frankness may be just what it takes to save you several hundred dollars in mortgage payments.

Or you might reply, "At 15 percent the building does not

make financial sense. It will be an alligator that I will have to feed each month." If you are going to use this approach, have your homework done. You will need to bring out your income and expense projections to show that your net operating income is not sufficient to pay the interest rate the seller is seeking.

Only one thing is certain. If you don't ask for a low interest rate, you won't get it. Make an offer at a rate lower than you think you'll get and then be willing to negotiate.

Amortization—Make Sure It Is Right for You

Once you determine the amount of interest on the loan, you must decide on the method of repayment. It is to the seller's advantage to have a fully amortized loan, since he gets a portion of his principal back with each payment you make as a buyer. Amortized loans were developed as a safety precaution for both buyers and sellers. Prior to the Great Depression of the 1930s, when many real estate loans made no provision for the reduction of principal through periodic payments, the person owing on a debt paid annual interest payments without reducing the principal amount. After the Depression, the weakness of this system became apparent. As a result, the current practice of principal reduction became standard procedure in the real estate industry.

Today, this type of loan calls for interest to be paid each month on the outstanding balance with an additional amount for the principal until the loan is paid off. When the payment is received, the interest due is first deducted and the balance of the payment is applied to reduce the principal.

For a number of years, most financial institutions offered fixed-rate twenty- and thirty-year fully amortized loans. Today, these loans are being replaced with various gimmicks aimed at adjusting the mortgages to follow the economic trends of the industry.

As a buyer, be sure to go over the numbers of a supposedly fully amortized loan. I have had several clients believe their notes were fully amortized, only to discover when they tried to sell their property that the loans actually demanded a balloon, or lump sum, payment. Many loans that are partially amortized appear to be fully amortized until you read the fine print and make a few calculations. Read the mortgages for trust deeds thoroughly before signing the assumption agreement. Better yet, let your attorney check them out.

Interest Only

In contrast to the fully amortized loan, you will come across the "interest only" loan. A far better deal for the buyer, this loan calls for monthly payments of interest only, while the balance remains constant, never decreasing. By paying interest only, the buyer reduces his monthly payments on the wraparound or carryback, thereby increasing his cash flow. Of course the loan eventually must be paid off. The seller is not going to wait forever.

Balloon—Stop—Call

The day of reckoning comes for everyone. If you have an interest-only loan, you know what day that will be. In the contract, along with the amount of the interest payment, you will find the clause, "With the entire balance due seven (7) years from close of escrow." It is a simple clause, yet it can be the most deadly aspect of the entire contract. With this clause you agree to pay off the entire loan at the end of the seventh year. Up until then, you will be making interest payments only. Where are you going to get the money for the payment? If you cannot come up with it, the person holding the note can have the building sold at an auction and you will probably lose everything you have in it.

Which brings me to two points. First, do not overextend yourself. Carefully check out the note you agree upon to determine if you can realistically meet the demands it sets forth. You can hope that income from the building will increase or that the economy will "turn around," but neither of these is a good risk. You have to work within *your* capabilities and be realistic. Second, planning is crucial to successful loan repayment.

Planning has to start early. That is why my illustration shows seven years. I will not accept any deal where I owe a lump sum of money due in less than seven years. In order to pay off the loan, I am going to need time to increase the value of my property and determine the right interest rate to charge a new buyer. I feel a seven-year period will give me the time I need. For me, three years or less is not enough time. I look around the country today and see many people who took out three-year notes in 1979 and 1980 who now may lose everything. They based their purchase on the principle that property values would continue to increase at the same rate they had for the previous three years. Their projections demonstrated a build-up of equity necessary to refinance the property at a savings and loan or bank and to pay off the short-term note. Unfortunately, few of these buyers knew or suspected that the market would slow down and even decline in certain cities, thereby reducing the borrowing power of the property.

Furthermore, as interest rates skyrocketed, more trouble set in. A building's net operating income can only cover so much in payments. When interest rates increase, the monthly payment also increases. This increase can very easily make the payment higher than the net operating income. If this is the case, no bank or savings and loan is going to give you a loan. They need to be assured that the building can handle the loan in the event that you do not make the payments and default. When negotiating the interest-only or balloon-payment loan, be *very* careful. Remember, the only one looking out for you is you.

Price *Versus* Interest Rate

Although you can negotiate both price and interest rate individually, it is important to understand the theory of decreasing interest and increasing price and vice versa.

Assume you have suggested an interest-only payment at a rate of 10 percent for $100,000. Assuming an $11,000 net operating income, you find yourself with $1,000 after paying for debt service. You consider $1,000 cash flow fair because you offered the seller $10,000 down and feel that 10 percent return, cash on cash, is fair.

The seller insists on 12 percent interest. This brings the interest amount to $12,000 and would produce a negative cash flow. The deal cannot be made.

Since there is only $10,000 to cover interest, the only alternative to the counter-offer is to lower the sales price and therefore lower the notes so that the $10,000 will cover the 12 percent interest. The note would have to be for $83,333 at 12 percent interest, instead of $100,000 at 10 percent, thereby lowering the price by $16,667. This could affect your tax position when you sell the property. However, as far as cash flow is concerned, the results will be the same.

The higher the interest rate, the lower the amount of the note and, conversely, the lower the interest rates the higher the note can be.

There is also a rule of "implied interest" which applies to the seller of property. This is the I.R.S.'s way of ensuring that sellers don't evade their tax liability by lowering interest rates too far. If the interest rate on a note or a contract for deed created by the seller is for anything less than 9 percent, the I.R.S. will imply an interest rate of 10 percent and tax the seller accordingly. The buyer, on the other hand, can write off a 10 percent interest payment for the year, even if his payment to the seller is actually less than that.

Due-on-Sale Clauses

Whenever you assume an existing loan, or take over the seller's payments at the bank, you do not even have to inform the bank. However, a wraparound exists where you create a new note to the seller and he remains responsible for his existing loans.

You must be aware of the "due-on-sale" clause. In the last few years, this clause alone has killed more deals than any other. It has appeared in most mortgages and trust deeds since the early Seventies. It states that the owner of the property may not sell all or any of the property without the lending institution's permission and that, should a sale take place, the institution shall have the right to accelerate the mortgage, requiring the seller to pay off the entire note.

Until the late Seventies, lending institutions did not enforce the clause because mortgage interest rates remained constant or increased only slightly. It was only when interest rates jumped drastically at the turn of the decade that lending institutions looked for ways to get out of the low-interest-rate loans and substitute higher yielding notes.

Each time the savings and loans or banks learned of a sale, they called the loan due and payable in an attempt to get the new buyer to come in and qualify for a new loan at a higher interest rate. This put the real estate market in a catch-22 position. If a buyer had to qualify for a new loan at a higher interest rate, the building would be an "alligator." This slowed down the sales of properties and as a result the lending institutions were still stuck with their low rates.

Buyers and sellers throughout the nation have since contested the constitutional right of lending institutions to enforce this clause. They claim it is an unfair restraint of trade. Each state court made its own ruling, some in favor of the banks and some in favor of the property owner. For the most part the state courts are favoring the owners. Their decisions are based on the fact that 1) the institution was not jeopardized by the sale and 2) the institution gained additional collateral because of the additional person or persons on the loan.

To complicate matters further the federal government issued a directive stating that federally chartered banks and savings institutions did not have to follow the state court decisions and could therefore accelerate their loans. Many claim that this ruling causes an unfair burden on the state-chartered institutions in the states where the property owner prevailed in court. A final decision was reached in Congress in October of 1982 with the Garn Act. The act created a three-year grace period for each state, but as of October 1985, they must all conform to the federal law favoring the banking institutions. (I will cover negotiating with the lending institution on this matter in chapter 13.)

At present, investors are trying a number of different ways to avoid due-on-sale clauses. I will discuss a few of them here, although I can not guarantee any of them. I only tell you about them and suggest you check with your attorney and/or C.P.A. before attempting any of them. They could backfire on you and you may end up having to qualify for a new loan that would quickly turn a good deal into a bad one.

1. Sell on a land contract or contract for deed or agreement for sale. In any of these transactions, legal title remains in the hands of the seller and it can be argued that no sale has taken place. The institutions argue that a sale is a sale even if title has not passed.

2. Many people are not informing the institutions of a sale and are transferring title and taking back a mortgage or trust deed under the same terms and conditions of the owner's mort-

gage. A third party is retained as a collection agency and this party pays the lending institution, thereby not alerting the institution by having a new party send checks for payment. The banks and savings and loans have become very aware of this attempt to deceive them, and are watching very carefully for a change of ownership on insurance policies. The institutions are even sending clerks to county recorders' offices to check on transfer of titles on properties that they have loans out on.

In 1980, a friend purchased an office building in Scottsdale, Arizona, and worked a wraparound trust deed with the seller to sidestep a higher interest rate from the bank. Fourteen months later, the bank caught on to the sale and sent notice of acceleration, that is, a letter informing the seller that the bank was aware of the sale and that unless the new owner would come in and qualify for the loan at the current interest rate, the bank would make the seller pay off the entire loan immediately!

Fortunately the seller and buyer had negotiated a clause into our contract that provided for the buyer to qualify for a new loan in the event that he was caught. When the letter came, the buyer simply had to negotiate with the bank for a new rate. He did, and the problem was corrected. Keep in mind that the bank does not really want to repossess the property. It is only trying to get a better rate on its loan, and is generally willing to work with you. Do not be fooled, however. If the bank decides to go through with an acceleration and for some reason you cannot qualify for a new loan, you could lose any interest you have in the property.

3. The family trust is another method being used by sellers to avoid the due-on-sale clause. The property is placed in a family trust, then the trust is sold to the buyer. This way the property does not change hands, since the trust would still be the actual owner. I recommend seeing your attorney before attempting this method. There are more complicated issues in trusts that have to be resolved, some of which I will describe later in this chapter.

The bottom line is this: There is a real problem with the due-on-sale clause and some very hard negotiating is going to be required to make a deal work if the clause is in the underlying encumbrance. Check to see whether the loan is assumable early in your negotiations. It may save you a great deal of time and energy.

Protect Your Interest

Selecting the financial instrument that will be used to secure your loan is a critical aspect of the negotiation. As you will see later in this chapter, the financial instrument you choose can also affect the way you take title. In some states a mortgage is actually a transfer of title to the real estate you purchase, as security for the payment of a debt. The seller conveys the property to the buyer subject to the terms of the mortgage. In other states, a mortgage is considered and treated strictly as a lien, which is when a person has a hold or claim on real property owned by someone as security for the debt.

Much like the purchase of a car, a lien is transferred to the buyer who takes possession of the premises as owner-debtor. Title transfers when he pays it off.

A deed of trust is used instead of a mortgage in these states: Arizona, California, Colorado, Idaho, Illinois, Minnesota, Mississippi, Missouri, New Mexico, North Carolina, Tennessee, Texas, Virginia, West Virginia, and the District of Columbia.

Essentially, a deed of trust is a mortgage giving the holder the power to sell the property upon default on the payments. Trust deeds have the same function as a mortgage except a mortgage names two parties, mortgagor and mortgagee, and a trust deed has three: trustor, trustee, and beneficiary.

If you have a mortgage on a property you have bought, then

you are the mortgagee and the lender is the mortgagor. On the other hand, if you use a deed of trust as security for your loan, you are the trustor, the lender is the beneficiary and the seller is the trustee. He still holds "naked" legal title to the property that is transferred to you by the deed of trust.

The most important difference between a mortgage and a deed of trust is in the method of foreclosure. Foreclosure under a trust deed usually takes a maximum of four months, although in some states it takes only thirty days. Once the sale takes place, the borrower loses all rights to redeem the property.

Conversely, foreclosure under a mortgage usually requires court proceedings and can take up to one and a half years. Then, after the foreclosure takes place, the borrower has a right of redemption for one year. Check your state for the exact amount of time of the right of redemption, if any.

This choice (when applicable) of course puts buyer and seller once again on opposite ends of the negotiation table. In short, most sellers prefer to use trust deeds rather than mortgages as security instruments because foreclosure is quicker and cheaper with a deed of trust. For obvious reasons then, a buyer should negotiate for a mortgage to protect his interest.

To clarify all this, let's look at some examples of how title is transferred under each of these instruments.

Legal Title With a Mortgage

The most common form of title transfer occurs when title passes subject to the current mortgages and the seller takes a junior mortgage for his equity. This instrument then becomes security for either a seller carryback or for a wraparound.

To illustrate, let's take the example of a building being sold under the following terms and follow it through different situations.

Purchase price = $100,000.
Current mortgage = $60,000 at 8 percent.
Down payment = $10,000.
Seller's equity = $30,000.

Situation A:

Seller and buyer agree to a carryback of $30,000 in the form of mortgage.

1. Title goes to the purchaser.
2. Purchaser assumes the $60,000 loan and the seller is either novated (to be novated is to have your name removed from the loan and to have no further responsibility) or he remains on the note.
3. Seller receives a note for $30,000 at terms agreed to by both parties. This note is secured by a junior mortgage in which the seller's security in the property is reduced by the amount of the first mortgage.

Should the buyer default on his payments, the seller may foreclose on the buyer. As I mentioned, this legal process can take up to eighteen months before the seller is satisfied, if ever. Furthermore, in the case of the missed payments, the seller will have to keep making the first-mortgage payments in order to protect his interest in the deal while he is taking legal action.

At the appropriate time, the court orders a foreclosure sale and the seller will have the opportunity to bid the amount of money owed, including legal fees and payments made to the first-mortgage holder. If no one else bids or the bids are lower, the seller is the owner of the property once again. If someone else bids higher than what the seller owes, then that one gets the property, the seller gets the money owed him, and the current owner gets the balance. In many states, if the seller gets less than what he is owed he may sue the owner for the difference.

Situation B

1. Seller agrees to a wraparound mortgage of 10 percent for $90,000.
2. Title transferred to purchaser.
3. Seller receives a note for $90,000 secured by a mortgage for $90,000 on the property.
4. Seller is responsible for underlying mortgage. In this situation, as in "A", the seller must also continue to pay on the underlying mortgage should the purchaser default, and the foreclosure procedure is the same.

In this case, the buyer should insist on a third-party collection agent to ensure that his payments are applied toward the senior mortgage. (See section on third-party clause, page 134.)

Although a mortgage takes a long time to foreclose there are advantages to the seller in this method. The primary advantage is that once the purchaser is late with a payment, the seller may insist that the entire loan be paid off. The purchaser does not have a choice to "cure" the deficiency as he does with other methods of sale. He must pay off the *entire* loan or lose the property.

Trust Deeds

As with a mortgage, a trust deed can also be used to secure a carryback or a wraparound. In this situation, the buyer is the trustor, the seller is the beneficiary, and the escrow company is the trustee.

When using this method the title goes to the purchaser. At the close of escrow the purchaser signs a trust deed in favor of the seller and names the escrow company as the trustee. The trustee is instructed to receive the payments from the purchaser and disburse to all the appropriate parties. When the last payment is made, the purchaser pays a small fee to the escrow company and the deed is reconveyed in full to the purchaser.

If, however, the purchaser is delinquent in his payments, the trustee, on instructions from the beneficiary (the seller), will start legal action toward forfeiture. This is done by giving notice to the purchaser that a trustee's sale will take place on a given day. The length of time before the sale will take place is set by each individual state. The purchaser has this period right up until the moment before the sale to cure the forfeiture, or to pay the back payments, interest, penalties, and legal fees incurred. If the buyer can do so, the seller has no recourse but to continue his contract. The purchaser can again become delinquent, in which case the seller would have to start over again with the forfeiture. If the payments are not made at the time of sale, a trustee's sale or auction takes place and the trustee sells the deed to the highest bidder. The beneficiary (seller) gets his money, including all interest and expenses, and the owner receives any additional funds. If this trust deed is a junior deed or a wraparound of another deed, the seller would have to continue making payments on the senior loans to protect his position and prevent a forfeiture by the loan holders. At the sale, the beneficiary is also entitled to receive any monies laid out for these payments.

Typically, the deed holder bids on his own property up to the amount of the deed. If no other bid is made, the seller would once again own the property.

It is apparent that this method favors the seller in that he can reclaim his property or get the money owed to him more quickly than by using the mortgage method. The buyer does have the advantage of being able to correct the deficiency by catching up on the late payments and not having to get a new loan. This way he is not required to pay the loan in full as long as it is paid on time.

In many states, mostly the western states, this method of lending is the most popular, though mortgages can still be used. In the states where mortgages are used, it is not illegal to use a trust deed, it is just not normal procedure. After reading about the trust deed as a buyer or seller you may prefer that route. Check with your attorney, though, to see if a trust deed really is to your advantage. The other party will also have to agree to this method.

title is free of tax & mechanic lienc.

When a Senior Loan Is Not a Senior Loan

Here is one loophole you must watch for: There are cases when a junior loan may be more junior than you thought.

The law states that your right to monies or equity in a property begins on the recorded date of your agreement, that is, the date your agreement is entered at the County Records Office. If you purchase a property and assume a mortgage on that deed from a seller, you will, of course, check the title. If you find that the only existing encumbrance is the mortgage or trust deed, you might assume you are secure. Unfortunately, there can be liens put on the property afterward which could preempt yours. If the seller had a tax problem or there were contractors who have done work on the property, they are legally able to place liens on the property. In most states, these liens would take a senior position to your ownership. In other words, if the seller has not paid off these liens you would have to pay them off to get clear title.

If you still owed the seller money, you could certainly deduct these costs from the amount due. But if you did not owe him anything, chances are slim that you will be able to get him to reimburse you. If he had the money he probably would have already paid the liens, so be careful.

Some years ago I bought a townhouse from a builder for $93,000, and assumed his $75,000 trust deed. Two months later the government slapped a tax lien on all of his properties and put them up for sale. I tried to negotiate this one out of the purchase, but could not. At the sale I was prepared to bid up to $93,000 to protect my interest. I had a cashier's check in my pocket and I was ready. But there were dozens of people present to bid on all of the units. My particular unit went for $97,000, higher than I cared to go. I lost the property, but got all of my money back because there was enough money remaining after the tax bill and the underlying loans were paid. I was lucky, but it could have worked out badly if I had not been able to qualify for a loan and the sales price was lower than the liens plus my equity. I won't make that mistake again and I hope you won't either!

Land Contracts, Agreements for Sale, Contracts for Deed

The names used may be different in each state, but the action and reaction is the same. Purchasing under these forms of ownership—land contracts, agreements for sale, contracts for deed—is a marked advantage for the seller and a marked disadvantage for the buyer.

As a buyer, you are purchasing property just as you might purchase an expensive toy at Christmas time: on a layaway plan. If the toy is priced at $100, you can pay $10 down and $10 a week. The store puts the toy away and when you make the last payment, you get the toy. If you stop making payments, the store will put it back on the shelf and sell it to someone else, keeping all of the money you have paid. The store never gave you the toy so it does not have to come and get it back. It is as simple as that.

Likewise, when you buy on a land contract, or on one of its forms, you do not get title until you pay off the contract. Title remains with the seller and if you are late with your payments, he can just give you notice that he is going to take it back. Each state will vary on the amount of time he has to notify you of default, and the time is generally based on how much equity you have in the property. But it is possible to end up losing a property in as little as thirty days. There is no redemption period and once it is lost, it is lost. All of your equity is gone.

It is also nearly impossible to borrow additional money against the property for improvements because very few lending institutions will loan money if they cannot put a lien on the property. Since you do not have title, you cannot sign any papers allowing the lien.

With these forms of purchasing, you would not have what is called *legal title.* What you do get is *equitable title,* which means that everything about ownership is yours except legal title. You get the interest deductions and the depreciation. You can collect the rent and you are liable for the expenses. Basically you are the owner of the property. It is just not in your name. You may wonder why anyone would want to buy this way, when everything is in the favor of the seller. Usually you do not want to buy this way, but you may agree to do so because of the other buyer benefits of the contract that have been discussed earlier in the book.

Many land contracts are written with little or no down payment. As a seller, you would not want to let the buyer "milk" the property for eighteen months while you foreclose on a mortgage. You would not want to give him even ninety days to default on your property. Remember, a purchaser with little or no money down might just walk away from a property if something goes wrong. By selling under a land contract however, as the seller and holder of the note you can step back in very quickly and minimize loss.

In 1973 I sold an office/apartment building on a land contract. The purchaser agreed to a very high price, about 20 percent over market value. He did not negotiate my original price. He agreed to pay the high price if I would give him the property with 5 percent down and five years to pay off the contract. During the five years, he would pay interest only and then he would pay off the entire balance on the due date.

Three months into the contract, he suffered financial setbacks

Sell for no $ down - use land contract.

and would not make the payments. I gave him notice of default and informed him that I would take back the property if I was not paid in the next thirty days. Fortunately for him and less fortunately for me, within two days of the deadline he found someone to take over for him and make the payments.

Should you elect to purchase property using this method, be sure you have reserve funds available to cover you, because you cannot be delinquent. Do not rely on the rents to come in on time. What if a tenant is late or you have vacancies? Under any other method of purchase you would most likely have time to correct it. But under a land contract, there is not enough time to fumble.

If you do purchase under this method, then negotiate for an option that would allow you to switch from this financing to one that is more secure. As a buyer, it would be to your benefit to do so.

Place a clause in the purchase agreement that calls for the land contract to be concluded after a period of time. Title is then to pass to the purchaser with a note going back to the seller secured by a mortgage or trust deed. The time period for this changeover could be one year or five years, depending upon when the seller finds he has enough of his equity out and the purchaser has enough cash into the deal to prevent him from walking away.

This agreement must be part of the initial contract talks. Once the land contract or contract for deed is signed, you as buyer will have no power to negotiate. You will be completely at the mercy of the seller, who will want to stay with the land contract. The only way you could then change it would be to pay off the contract or renegotiate with the seller. Then you will probably face a higher interest rate or have to pay more cash.

The way in which a sale is made and financed can drastically affect the safety of the investment for each party. If people devoted more time to this aspect of real estate negotiations, we would have happier buyers and sellers. Whether you choose a mortgage, trust deed, or land contract, it is important to consult your attorney, establish your goals as a buyer or seller, and decide *before* you sign how much you will compromise.

You must negotiate from strength. You have little strength once you have signed the agreements.

The Fine Points Can
Save You Thousands

In the previous chapters we discussed the major elements of contract writing. Now it's time to work out the minor details, those nitty gritty points that can be used as tools to work for you or against you. Many people think the small points are only a series of blanks to be filled in with standard, traditional phrases. This needn't be the case. The rest of the contract may provide the opportunity to save thousands of dollars. A basic transaction may seem straightforward and standard. But as you now understand, no contract is "standard." Each can and should be molded and shaped to fit your specific goals.

Personal Property and Land as Part of the Purchase Price

Rarely do we see a breakdown of the purchase price in an offer or acceptance, yet as a buyer you could save many dollars by assigning separate values to the land, personal property, and building. Let's say you buy four furnished units for $160,000. Your analysis reveals the land to be worth $20,000, the furniture and appliances worth $24,000, and the building valued at $116,000.

In the body of the contract, there should be a clause that reads: "Purchase price to be $160,000. This price includes $20,-000 for the land, $24,000 for the personal property, and $116,-000 for the building." In this way, you establish a tax basis for depreciation. Depreciation is the paper loss most people try to establish through the purchase of real estate. Of course your friendly I.R.S. agent would like nothing better than to reduce the amount of deductions. But if the buyer and the seller agree to $24,000 for the personal property, and the number is a reasonable one, it will be very difficult for the I.R.S. to question the figure. Likewise, if a fair market value is also established for the land, the remainder of the purchase price ($116,000 in our case) is allocated to the building's value, and established as its tax basis.

Although this clause seems innocent enough to the buyer, it could be very costly to the seller. Should he agree to a fair market value of $24,000 for the furniture, he is admitting the sale of the furniture for that price. If, over the years of ownership, he has depreciated the personal property below the $24,000 amount, he will be subject to a recapture tax. That is, he will have to pay an ordinary income tax on the difference instead of declaring all of the profits a long-term capital gain. Armed with this knowledge, most sellers who are aware of this point will generally refuse to add the clause. The seller's accountant registers the furniture as the seller's gift of valueless personal property and does not recapture any gain. The purchaser's accountant will depreciate the furniture from a basis of $24,000. However, if one or the other is audited, the buyer and seller could be required to adjust their deductions so that their claims agree.

Condition of Personal Property

The condition of the personal property is another item for negotiation. The seller would prefer to sell the property in an "as is" condition or based on a "buyer beware" basis. Once this kind of deal has closed, the property belongs to the buyer, and so do the headaches. For a buyer this is the worst method of purchase. Your best choice would be to include a clause that states: "The seller warrants the condition of the property for a period of one year from close of escrow." However, not too many sellers will concede to this clause, unless it is a small apartment complex or single-family home and the seller can get a home warranty insurance policy on the property. If you are the seller, use the "as is" condition with caution. A few courts have viewed this term to be misleading and several purchasers have gone to court claiming they didn't know what "as is" meant. If you do attempt to sell the property in an "as is" condition then rephrase your clause to read: "Buyer has examined the property and, being knowledgeable in the field, does agree to take the property in an 'as is' condition." This may provide more protection for you.

Prepayment Penalties

As a buyer, you'll have monthly payments to make. You may have an interest-only loan with a balloon payment due sometime in the future, or you may have a fully amortized loan with monthly payments of principal and interest. Unless there is a balloon date, the amortized loan will eventually pay off. Occasionally you may desire to pay the loan off earlier. Perhaps the equity increases because the value of the property appreciates and you wish to borrow a larger amount without taking a second mortgage. Or better yet, maybe interest rates on loans have dropped and you can negotiate a better interest rate on a new loan. Or you may find that your second loan has a balloon coming due and the only way you can cover it is to pay off both the first and second loan with a new mortgage.

All of the above situations require an advance payment on the outstanding loan.

As a buyer, you can ensure the right to make additional

payments without a penalty by adding the words "or more" to your contract right after the clause on payments. For example: "Payments shall be $323.33, or more, each month, beginning thirty days after closing." Unless there is a specific clause placed in the contract by the seller to negate your privilege you have the right to make additional principal payments at no extra charge.

On the other hand, as a seller you may have reasons for why you would not want advanced payments from the buyer. Suppose you just sold a building and have agreed to carryback a note for $100,000. The contract calls for the buyer to make interest-only payments to you at 15 percent over the next five years, with the entire balance due five years from closing. You are going to receive $15,000 per year in interest, and you have structured your tax deductions to cover the income. If the purchaser were to give you $100,000 in December of any year, you wouldn't have time to make wise investments to cover the concurrent tax liability and you would see much of your profits going to Uncle Sam. To prevent this you must place a "lock-in" term on the buyer, stating that he cannot pay more than a given amount during any year.

In 1978, I was involved in a twenty-four-unit resort complex transaction where the seller had a similar problem. He worded the contract to state: "Purchaser may not pay any additional funds in 1979 nor more than one-third of the outstanding balance in 1981." This prevented him from getting a windfall of cash and paying too much tax.

You should also be aware that banks, savings and loans, and insurance companies may also include contract "lock-ins" and prepayment penalties. Although some states have outlawed prepayment penalties, this right still exists in many states. Planning on long range investments, these institutions will charge as much as six months worth of interest for paying off a loan early.

I know of a case where an insurance company put a ten-year lock-in clause in a note secured by a trust deed and then added a participation clause for which they would receive 15 percent of all gross rent above $330,000 per annum. In 1974, the owner didn't think it was much of a problem because the rent would have to climb from $190,000 to $330,000 before he would be affected. No one planned on the inflation we experienced from 1974 to 1979, and in 1978, after rents skyrocketed, the insurance company was at the owner's door seeking its pound of flesh. The seller had no choice but to pay the insurance company through 1984.

Remedy for Not Closing

Unfortunately, deals go bad. Some never get off the ground, and some go bad after they close. A deal can fall through for any number of reasons, most commonly when one party or the other backs out. Perhaps the income and expenses did not balance as promised. The transaction might fall through after the physical inspection of the property or because the purchaser lacks the funds necessary to close. There are hundreds of reasons for a deal not to go through. When it does fail, one side usually calls foul. Generally, the seller is suffering financial loss. The canceling of the deal can have a domino effect on many other deals and many people can suffer. When this happens, someone always demands recourse.

If the buyer cancels the contract during the contingency period while he is making inspections of the books, records, and so on, then the earnest money is returned in full and everyone goes about his own business in a normal manner. On the other hand, if the seller terminates any time prior to the buyer's removing all of the contingencies, then the buyer may have legitimate grounds to demand recourse.

Let's look at the situations you may find yourself in. As a buyer, there are two possibilities:

1. You are the buyer, and you want out. Either you couldn't come up with the money, or you found a better property. In this case, you would like the penalty to be a loss of your earnest deposit and nothing else.

2. You are the buyer and the seller wants out. In this situation the seller may have decided to keep the property, or has discovered he can get a better price from you or from someone else.

Under these circumstances, you want him to complete the deal, so you want the right to demand "specific performance," which demands that he live up to the deal.

As the seller there are also two possibilities:

1. You are the seller and the buyer wants out. In this case, you want the deal to close but the buyer may have found a better property to purchase and you may have lost other potential buyers as a result of having your property tied up. You want the contract to read that you have the right, by law, to require specific performance, forcing the buyer to go through with the deal.

2. You are the seller and you want out. You would like to give all earnest money back to the purchaser and declare that the offer is null and void.

In most "standard agreements," unless you make prior changes, both parties can be forced to complete the transaction in a court of law. If at all possible, remove the clause if it goes contrary to your position. Otherwise, it could tie up the property for years and cost a great deal of your time and money to settle the issue.

Security Deposits

A security deposit is another item that is rarely discussed in the contract. It should always be included, however, or both the buyer and the seller might run into problems.

There are two different types of security deposits to be covered.
1. *Refundable.* A tenant moves into the apartment complex and is charged anywhere from $100 to a full month's rent as a refundable deposit. If the tenant pays his rent on time, cleans up when he leaves, and doesn't do any damage, he is entitled to a full refund. If a problem does arise, the owner may keep a portion of the deposit to cover damages. Since the money is returnable to the tenant and since the new owner assumes the responsibility for returning it, it is logical to assume the purchaser should be given credit for the deposits at closing. If the contract is silent, that is, makes no mention of it, the escrow officer usually will transfer the deposits from seller to buyer, simply as a matter of tradition.

You may be surprised to learn that it is not always necessary to transfer the deposits. In one transaction I was involved in, the seller made it clear that he was keeping the deposits, even though I would have to return the money to the tenants when they moved out. I wasn't concerned. I simply added the lost deposits to the purchase price and made my offer based on that total.

2. *Nonrefundable.* This second type of security deposit is illegal in some states, but is still used widely throughout most of the country. Called a "move-in fee," "key fee," "non-refundable deposit," "decorating fee," or any other name, it is a landlord rip-off. It is a one-time charge made to the new tenant and is not refundable. It is a way to increase income. The decision as to who gets credit for this portion of the de-

posit is even more ambiguous than for a refundable deposit.

As a seller you can argue that you wanted the money when the tenant moved in and that there is nothing left to pass on to the buyer. If I were the purchaser, I would challenge this concept. Since the apartment will need to be cleaned when the tenant vacates, the deposit should be transferable.

The matter of who "owns" deposits is not clear under the law either, so the best advice I can give is to negotiate and have the terms written into the contract before closing.

Prepaid Rent

You should always include a clause pertaining to prepaid rent in the contract. Since the tenant pays rent in advance (generally 30 days or one month), it seems logical to assume that the seller keep all rent money paid up to the day of closing and the buyer get credit or cash for any prepaid days after closing, yet there is no law or rule as to what happens. Be aware that the title company will prorate the rent based on the day of closing unless you have stipulated otherwise in the contract. If the contract is silent, then the seller should retain all rent collected regardless of the period it covers. The only time rent should be prorated to the purchaser is when it is specifically called for in the contract. For example, you are the seller of a building on which rent is $300 per month ($10 per day). If you collect the full $300 rent on the first of the month and sell the building on the tenth, the normal thing to do would be for the seller to give the buyer $200 credit for the remaining 20 days. But if there is no proration agreement specified in the contract, the seller can keep it all and the buyer gets nothing from his tenant for the 20 days.

You can benefit from the mistakes made by the opposition; be especially aware of the timing of the close of the transaction. If you are the seller and there is no mention of proration of rents, then a closing on the fourth or fifth would be ideal. You would have to pay expenses for four or five days, but you would receive rents for the entire month and the buyer would have to wait until next month for his first collection.

As a buyer, if there is no proration, you would come out best with a closing on the last day of the month, enabling you to collect rent the next day, assuming that rent is due on the first. If it is due at any other time, then you would adjust your plan accordingly.

There is another type of prepaid rent that buyers often overlook. Many landlords collect the first and last months rent when a tenant moves in to protect themselves in case a tenant moves out suddenly without paying. Logically, this money belongs to the purchaser since he will own the building during the tenant's last month, when rent will not be paid. Again, although this is logical, it is not automatic. Unless the buyer reads the leases or covers his bases in the contract, he is out of luck. Once the deal closes, the seller has no obligation to give credit to the buyer.

Taxes

You will also have to decide whether it is in your best interests to have real estate taxes prorated. Taxes are paid in advance in some states and in others they are paid in arrears. How they are paid and when they are due is very relevant to your negotiations. If taxes are paid after the fact it is to the seller's advantage to have the contract silent on this matter because the buyer will have to pay the tax bill when it becomes due. It would be to the purchaser's benefit to include in his offer that "all taxes will be prorated to the day of closing."

On the other hand, if the taxes are paid in advance, the opposite is true. The purchaser will try to ignore any discussion of taxes and the seller will want to make sure the taxes are prorated.

Insurance

Insurance is often combined with the taxes so that the contract clause reads "taxes and insurance to be prorated to the day of closing." This is not a good idea. I advise you to keep them separate, because insurance can be a tricky item. As we stated in chapter 5, you will probably want to get a new insurance policy. This does not prohibit your receiving credit for your money at closing. But, if the clause is left the normal way and the seller has paid through the end of December for his insurance, and you buy the property on July 1, you will owe the seller for six months of insurance and you may end up with a policy you don't want. On the other hand, if you don't request proration, you will not get the option of the less expensive policy if you want it. The best way to handle this is first to find out when the insurance is paid through; if there is substantial time remaining on the policy after the closing date, request "policy to be given to buyer at closing at no charge."

I have been involved in contracts where the buyer requests that the seller "throw in the insurance policy for the balance of the year," and I have seen contracts requiring the buyer to pay back the seller on a prorated basis for the prepaid portion of the policy. There is no standard and it is wise to investigate your options and negotiate for what is best for you in each case.

If you are a seller, the issue of insurance may be one battle you are willing to lose in exchange for a victory somewhere else in the contract. If you put in "purchaser to prorate," you will get compensated, but you could just as easily state, "purchaser to provide own policy at closing" and you will receive a credit from your agent at closing for the unused portion. But first, check with your agent. You might find out you will receive less than you feel you are entitled to because of the insurance carrier's refund policy. Often, they keep a percentage of the unused portion as a service fee for policy cancellations. If this is the case with your policy you may want to give the balance of the year away free, especially if it covers only a couple of months. The purchaser might think he has won something and will concede another item in the contract to you.

Impounds

Each time we write a contract we are sure of two things. If payments are made, everything will go along smoothly, and if payments are not made, something bad will happen. This is not only true for the underlying encumbrances, but is also true for the taxes and insurance.

If the buyer doesn't pay the taxes, it is possible the building will be sold by the state. If you have an equity position in the property due to a carryback or a wraparound, you stand the chance of losing everything. If the building caught fire and the purchaser didn't have insurance you would also be the loser. In either case, you could also be liable to the underlying lien holders. To protect yourself as a seller, ask that the purchaser include with his monthly payment, "one-half of the annual taxes and insurance." If a collection agent is handling the payments, it will hold the excess each month and pay the tax bill to the state and the premiums to the insurance company when they come due. This fund held is called an "impound account." As a purchaser, however, you don't want the clause in the contract. Why should someone else have use of your money for a year at a time?

Of course, there are times when this item is not negotiable. If you are assuming an already existing loan and the lender has the clause in the note, then you must live with it. With any Veterans Association or Federal Housing Authority loan, it is a required item. Banks and savings and loans will make you think it non-negotiable, but it is as negotiable as the interest rate or points. If you are dealing with a free and clear piece of real estate or with a private lender, there is a good chance it can be left out of the contract. Many sellers try to get it back in the deal after the closing through the escrow company, but you don't have to go along with it.

Since insurance and taxes are negotiable items, there is more to negotiate than whether or not you as a buyer will pay them monthly. If you do agree, you should request in turn that "the funds be placed in an interest-bearing account with the interest accruing for your benefit." At least you will get a little something for your effort and your money won't be tied up worthlessly.

Late Payments

If you make a mortgage payment on the fifteenth and it was due on the first, the chances are you will have to pay a late payment penalty depending upon what is in the standard agreement. Be very careful about making your payments on time.

I have seen a charge of 4 percent of the payment ($40 on a $1,000-a-month payment) and I have seen a clause where the interest on the entire note goes from 12 percent (the interest called for) to 18 percent from the day the payment was due until paid. On a $100,000 loan with $1,000 monthly payments, this could jump to $1,500 for a one-month delinquency. Beware of this clause even though it looks harmless. You may be confident that you are going to make your payments, and not worry about it. But, be prepared for the times when you may be late.

leave it in

Many sellers leave this clause out of the contract. Since you are not used to being a lender, you do not think as a lender. The clause is a standard item in contracts written by lending institutions, but for most private investors it is something new.

Early in my contract-writing days, I sold a triplex on a wraparound agreement at 9 percent and I remained responsible for the underlying 6½ percent mortgage. I forgot to add a late-payment penalty into my contract and, true to Murphy's law, this was the loan that developed a payment problem and became delinquent.

The buyer didn't pay me, yet I had to continue to make the mortgage payments while at the same time taking legal action against the purchaser. This put me in a financial bind and as a result I was often late with my payments. The bank was sympathetic but still insisted on their late fee. Three months later the buyer was able to catch up on his payments, but when I asked for the late charges, he refused, stating that there was no provision for payments of late fees in his contract. He was right. He hadn't assumed my mortgage so he was not responsible for any of the terms. His only agreement was with me. Since I had not specified a late payment penalty in the contract, I received nothing.

Include a Subordination

You should have a subordination clause in your contract, one that is fair to both buyer and seller. I do not mean here the type of subordination clauses that allows unsuspecting people to be conned out of their equity. Sharks without scruples persuade them to pledge their free and clear property for a building project and then, when the proposed project falls through, the con artists walk away from the deal and the banks and savings and loans end up with the property.

The fair subordination clause that I recommend should not cause any problems to either party, but it is often necessary to the purchaser to make the deal fly.

Assume you agree to purchase a building for a total price of $80,000. You put $10,000 down, assume a $50,000, 8 percent loan that is due in five years, and the seller carries the remaining $20,000 at 10 percent interest only, with the entire balance due in seven years. The $50,000 loan becomes a senior loan and the $20,000 a junior loan. In five years, you will have to cover the $50,000 by either selling the property or refinancing it.

Without a subordination clause, any new loan you put on the property, even one to pay off the old loan, would become junior to the $20,000 note. If you paid off the $50,000 loan with a new $50,000 loan, the $20,000 would become the senior loan and the $50,000 the junior. This makes lenders a little uneasy. It will be very difficult to borrow $50,000 if it will be in a junior position on the $80,000 property. Even if it could be done, the interest rate on a second loan would be much higher than on the first loan. To prevent this problem you will need to insert a clause that reads: "Seller's encumbrance of $20,000 shall be subordinate to the current loan of $50,000 and to any replacement or extension of said loan." The seller has now given you the right to refinance the $50,000 as a senior note and has agreed to leave his note in second position.

Permission to Show Property

From time to time, the property you will be purchasing will be vacant or become vacant during the closing period. If you are purchasing a single-family home or duplex that is currently owner-occupied, it may become vacant when you assume title.

If this happens, it could take months to find a tenant, during which time you'll have an alligator. To avoid this problem, include a clause in the contract that states: "Purchaser has right to show property to prospective tenants during escrow period." (If you are in an escrow state.) This will accomplish two things. First, it will give you the chance to see if you can obtain a tenant prior to closing. And second, it may help you find out if you have a good deal. If you advertise the property for rent during the closing period and can't negotiate a lease at a necessary price, you may decide your deal wasn't as good as you thought.

At this point you may want to make use of your weasel clause to back out of the deal and request return of your earnest deposit. Even if the contingency period is over, it might still be better to forfeit your earnest deposit and walk away from the deal rather than throw good money after bad. If you make a bad deal, accept the fact. Take your loss, but keep it small. We all make bad judgments now and then, but if you can keep your occasional losses small and your gains large, you'll always come out ahead.

Another reason to negotiate the "permission to show property" clause into the contract is to enable you to show the property to prospective buyers of the property. If you have negotiated a sound deal, there may be an opportunity to sell the property before you close on it. But of course, anyone interested in buying it would want to examine the property, and this clause would enable others to inspect the property prior to purchase.

A word of caution is required here. In your contract to lease or rent to another party, make sure there is a "hedge clause" stating that the contract or lease is based upon your obtaining the property, and that should you not close, the lease or contract is void. This will get you out of any tight spots.

Termite Inspection

Many standard contracts leave out a clause handling termite or insect inspection. The absence of this clause can be very costly to the buyer.

In 1976, I purchased a two-year-old office building made of frame and stucco that appeared to be in good condition. Many of the units had not yet been decorated or rented. For all practical purposes the building was brand new. The probability of termite infestation was so remote that the seller did not mind a clause calling for "seller to provide a termite inspection report from a licensed pest control company and to repair, prior to close of escrow, any damage created by any type of insect infestation." Twenty-four hundred dollars later, he completed the termite repair and I had my building. Apparently, the builder had not treated the wood prior to construction and there had been a serious termite problem. When you are doing the physical inspection yourself, beware of areas that are covered up. Shelves with contact paper are a good example. Sellers will do cosmetic repairs without getting rid of a problem and then hide the patchwork with attractive coverings.

1031 Tax-Deferred Exchange Clause

Even if you have no intention to exchange one property for another, you should include this clause in your contract. A 1031 tax-deferred exchange allows an owner of a property to exchange it for a like property, providing he meets certain I.R.S. regulations. The exchange transaction will be less trouble to both buyer and seller if the proper clause is included: "Each party to this transaction agrees to participate in a 1031 tax-deferred exchange at the cost and risk of the party benefiting by the exchange, provided the 1031 exchange does not delay the closing of the transaction."

In essence, the clause accomplishes two things. First it notifies all parties that a tax-deferred exchange is involved and that their participation is required. Second, the clause demonstrates "intent" to the I.R.S. In order to qualify for the benefits of a tax-deferred exchange you must show intent to exchange the property from the onset of the transaction (as opposed to outright sale). To include the clause at a later date—or not at all—may jeopardize your exchange classification by the I.R.S. and have it ruled as an outright sale regardless of the fact that an exchange occurred. The important point is to show intent to exchange, otherwise the taxes due on the transaction could be more than you anticipated.

Of course, this clause does not *require* you to exchange, it simply allows either party to utilize the favorable ruling if they choose to. One party could be taking advantage of an exchange while the other is selling outright. Any additional costs associated with the exchange are the sole responsibility of the party benefiting from the exchange. Since this is a complex issue, I suggest you get additional information from your accountant.

Nonrecourse

Everyone who invests in real estate worries about investing heavily in a property and then discovering it was a mistake. Not only could you lose your investment, but you could also lose everything you've worked for: your home, car, business—in fact, all of your valued assets.

In order to prevent this from happening, you may want to include a nonrecourse or exculpatory clause in your offer: "The liability shall be limited to the property itself and shall not extend beyond this." This prevents anyone with a lien on your property from getting any more than he could receive from a foreclosure sale of the property. Under normal circumstances, without the clause, a lender can have the property sold to recover his loss if you fail to pay. If an auction on the property doesn't bring enough money to recover the debt, the lender has the right to obtain a deficiency judgment against you, enabling him to attack all of your other assets in order to recover the balance due.

Certain states have this clause built into their state statutes on single-family homes. These laws have been instituted to protect home buyers. If they should lose their house, they will still retain their other assets. But in the states where these laws have been passed, they only apply to owner-occupied dwellings, not residential or commercial income property, so you should include the clause in all of your contracts.

Inventory

Earlier, we discussed the matter of depreciating personal property; but how can you be sure that all the personal property you agreed to buy will be transferred at closing? Many times the seller will substitute older or cheaper furniture and appliances for the items you saw during the inspection.

To prevent this, you may want to take pictures of the various rooms or units and ask for a note stipulating that all of the personal property now on the premises and used in the normal operation of the building and owned by the seller will be part of the transaction. Include an inventory clause such as: "Seller to provide itemized list of all personal property prior to removal of contingencies." By doing so you are covering all your bases.

Right to Accompany Agent

Too often your real estate agent ends up being a "Pedro." Most of the time it's not intentional, but caused by misunderstanding. The agent has been taught that a buyer and seller should be kept apart in residential transactions. Emotions often run high and if either party is confronted by the other, the deal could fall through because of an accidental insult or snide remark about the house. Yet, when dealing with income property, an entirely different situation arises. Emotions are not part of the transaction. Buyer and seller are concerned with profits, and price is determined by net operating income, gross rent multiplier, net rent multiplier, and other financial formulas. Therefore, uniting buyer and seller can only help the negotiation process, and as we discussed in chapter 2, you should accompany your agent to the negotiating table.

Zoning

Zoning may not seem important when buying a pre-existing property. But don't be deceived by assuming a property is zoned for its current use. "This offer contingent upon the property being zoned (XXX)" is a clause that could keep you out of a great deal of trouble. A woman in Richardson, Texas, purchased a fourplex with the intention to live in one unit and rent the other three to cover costs. Three months after the purchase, a city official informed her that the property was zoned strictly for a duplex and that the operation of a fourplex would be disallowed. Apparently a few neighbors had complained. A thorough examination revealed that the previous owner had illegally converted a single-family home into a four-

plex, sold it as a fourplex, and then moved away. The woman
had no recourse. Unable to find the seller, she was forced to take
a loss and feed a large hungry alligator. She could have prevented this by simply checking the zoning prior to removal of
contingencies.

Zoning can be very mysterious. We have an office building
in Phoenix which was the headquarters for my company until
we leased ourselves out of the building. After being there for
two years, I discovered that a real estate company was not an
acceptable tenant under a C-1 zoning regulation. It was all right
to have an insurance company, but not a real estate company.
When checking with the city officials for an explanation, I
discovered that real estate offices are more active and have more
traffic than do insurance companies and thus different zoning
is indicated.

This brings up another point. Check to see if your tenants'
activities are legal, whether you are purchasing a strip joint or
an office building. Do not accept anything as fact unless you
have checked it. And once again, make sure you have that
weasel clause to get out of the deal if it does not meet with your
approval.

Financing

The all-inclusive weasel clause covers practically everything
except financing. It enables you to review the current financing,
but doesn't allow for the situation that requires a specific loan
from a financial institution. In this case add an additional clause
specifying the type of loan you will need to get. For example:
"This offer contingent upon obtaining financing at not more
than 11 percent per annum, with a twenty-five-year amortiza-
tion, with the entire balance due in no less than ten years."

This sets the minimum standard you will accept and gives

you the right to back out without penalty should you not be able to get those terms.

It is impossible to cover every single item that should be included in a contract based on your specific purchase or sale, but I have given you the most common ones. For the most part, any other problem can be covered under the all-inclusive weasel clause. If you think something was left out of the contract, just exercise your rights under the weasel clause unless the seller is willing to negotiate your new requirements.

CHAPTER
11

Landlord-Tenant
Negotiations

Your real estate negotiations will not be limited to dealing with buyers and sellers. Once you purchase your property it will be necessary to apply various methods and techniques to negotiate with the tenants in the building. Negotiation is a tool anyone can learn to use effectively in landlord-tenant situations. If you're willing to practice, you can translate your knowledge into a system that recognizes needs and applies the appropriate tactics to meet those needs.

As an owner and, if you manage your own property, as a landlord, you will have to wear many hats. To get the prospective tenants to rent, you must be a salesman; to settle disputes between tenants, you'll need to be a judge; to keep tenants in line, you'll have to be a peace officer; to collect your rents on time, you will have to be a scrooge.

So in this chapter we will consider some negotiation tactics to assist the relationship with your renters and develop your ability to handle them as a seasoned negotiator.

The Salesman

Assuming you have placed a good ad in the newspaper or used some other method to get people to call, you now must become a super salesman to get people to your property. You are competing with several other apartment owners who also have vacancies and you must show a potential renter why your units are better than others.

Before the phone even rings in answer to your ad you must mentally prepare for the upcoming challenge. Have paper and pencil ready to write down information. Have a list of prequalifying questions such as: What size apartment do you need? Do you have children? Pets? Where are you employed? How long have you been in town?

Then when the phone rings look into a nearby mirror and smile. Believe it or not your smile will project through the phone when you say "hello." Take a positive attitude regarding your apartment and SELL. Let your enthusiasm flow through the phone to the prospects. This will make them want to see your units.

To begin with, it will be helpful to you to address your potential renters as "residents." This will set the stage toward getting your way in negotiations. People do not mind being called "residents," yet when they are addressed as "tenants," they immediately take a defensive position, and bargaining with them becomes much more difficult. The word "tenant" is often associated with poverty or lower class. This originates from the inner-city slums where residents of tenement houses were called tenants, and the word still holds a negative connotation today.

To negotiate an appointment to see your property, take an aggressive position. Give each caller the impression that you are genuinely concerned about him becoming your resident. He must feel he is the most important person you have talked to all day.

After describing the apartment or house and answering minor questions, make an appointment to get the "prospect" to the unit. He will not rent anything over the phone so don't try to sell the dwelling on the phone. Just sell the appointment. Go for the "two choice close" by suggesting two times when it would be convenient to show him the unit.

You might suggest, "Would three o'clock this afternoon be good for you or would ten in the morning be better." This is part of the "win-win" form of asking questions. Either answer is right for you.

Initial Impression

Remember that during your talks with prospective residents negotiations are not only verbal; there are nonverbal negotiations occurring all the time. If you are to negotiate the rental of your property to a successful conclusion, you need to first take the necessary steps to set the stage. The initial impression of the property goes a long way toward making or breaking the deal. Generally you meet the prospect at the site. What he sees as he drives up could make the difference between an empty unit and an occupied one.

I had a friend call one day with a puzzling problem. He ran a great ad in the paper, received thirteen phone calls and set up six appointments, each fifteen minutes apart, to show his vacant apartment. At the site he waited two hours; no one showed up. Not one of the six appeared or called to cancel. "What happened?" was his question to me.

The answer was obvious, without even going to the site. He thought I was a mind reader when, without seeing the property, I described it perfectly: run-down, full garbage cans, dirty papers and empty cans throughout, and a general all-around unkempt appearance, especially in the front of the building, where the prospect makes his initial contact.

I explained that in all probability most, if not all, of the prospects came for the appointment, but kept right on going, after taking a look at the property. He cleaned up the outside, reran the ad and had the unit rented in a week.

First impressions are tremendously important. The route you give to get to your site is very important. If there is a choice, make sure you direct people to take the simplest and most scenic way possible.

I lived on a mountain in Paradise Valley, Arizona, with $250,000 to $400,000 homes below me and $1,000,000 houses above me. When showing my house to prospective buyers I directed them the longer way around, past the higher-priced houses rather than sending them the shorter route through the lower-priced homes.

You will also have to be sure the building is in good condition inside as well. A dirty apartment or house or a musty smelling unit is an immediate turn-off. Don't show a unit before it is ready. Make sure it is cleaned up, especially the kitchen and bathroom.

As for eliminating that musty smell that appears in most vacant units around the country, try putting a few drops of vanilla extract on one of the burners of the electric range fifteen minutes before the appointment. Turn the burner on and soon the place will have the aroma of freshly baked cookies. If you have a gas stove, you'll have to use a light bulb instead. Apply the extract before you turn the light on to minimize the risk of cracking the bulb.

Do Not Give out the Key

It's impossible to negotiate with a prospective tenant when you don't get to talk to him. Yet if you give a key to a prospect and let him look at the property alone, that would be just what you were doing.

When prospects go off by themselves, they will find every-thing wrong with the apartment. They will even find things wrong that aren't wrong. The color of the paint will be wrong. The rooms too small. The refrigerator too old. They'll claim the carpet is too dirty, etc. You won't stand a chance. You must go with the prospects and lead them through the unit. Also, use subtle negotiation techniques while showing them through. Explain that the carpet will be cleaned before they move in and you will paint the apartment if they sign a lease today. Explain that the money you will be saving on having a tenant and not having to advertise will be passed on to them.

Emphasize the positive features and downplay the negative ones. "I realize the second bedroom is a little small, however, the view from the window, overlooking the mountains and the tennis court, is magnificent!" That way you are negotiating a give-and-take compromise.

A realtor used this tactic perfectly on me, when I purchased a condominium in Hawaii. As we stepped onto the balcony we could barely see the ocean through all of the hotels blocking the view. Yet the realtor emphasized the beautiful view of Diamond Head, and as an added bonus we had a "peek" at the ocean. He took a negative and turned it into a strong positive.

After the future tenants look at the property the next step is their's. If they say they want it, it's up to you. You have to decide if you want them and if you are willing to go along with any concessions they are requesting.

Suppose they ask for a new refrigerator before they will move in. Are they worth the extra cost? Can you negotiate a lesser amount? Perhaps you can get them to pay $10 more per month if you buy a new refrigerator. Will they settle for a different used refrigerator? How long will the unit stay open if you don't rent to this tenant? One day, one week, one month!? Is a new refrigerator a cheap price to pay for a tenant now?

The same principles of negotiating with a seller apply here. You must set your limits and stick to them. If you have set $150 as the maximum expenditure to get the apartment rented, don't exceed that limit, no matter how tempting it becomes.

What if You Don't Want Them?

Now that you know all the right things to do, you have to learn all the wrong things to do! Why? Because you are going to run into some prospects that you don't want as tenants. Remember, it is better to have no tenant than to have a bad tenant. At least with no tenant you don't have wear and tear on the unit and you are not running up utility bills. With a bad tenant you have a no-win situation. You can't show the unit while it is occupied and you'll probably have to go through the court system to get him out. The money you'll lose will teach you to be more careful the next time.

If you do decide you don't want a prospect, do everything you can to discourage him. When he asks about children and you know he doesn't have any, let him know about how great it is at the complex for all the little kids running around. Talk about the play area and how the mothers get together at the pool each afternoon and take the kids swimming.

If people inquire about noise at night it is generally because they are looking for a quiet place to live. Tell them the trucks don't make too much noise when they pass by and most of the tenants, with the exception of the two in apartment 6, turn down their stereos by midnight. That should scare them away.

If for some reason the reverse-sell tactic doesn't work, you will have to resort to other methods. You can always fail to approve them because of their credit rating or because of what you learned from their previous landlords, but the best method I have ever seen or heard is one that was taught to me by Dr. Albert J. Lowry, who did more for the new landlord than anyone in his book *How to Manage Real Estate in Your Spare Time.* He suggests you make an unexpected visit to the current residence of your prospective tenants with their deposit in one pocket and the key to their new apartment in the other. You mention to them when they answer the door that you wanted to talk to them about their application. The real reason for the visit, however, is to see how they live. They will not change their habits when they move into your unit.

If, after looking around, you are happy with them, you reach into your pocket, produce the key and say, "Congratulations, here is the key to your apartment." On the other hand if you are dissatisfied and don't want them as your tenants, reach into your other pocket and produce their deposit and give it back apologetically stating, "I'm sorry, but you weren't accepted."

Structuring Your Rental Agreement

Negotiation comes in many shapes and forms. One item that is not considered too often is the cost of negotiating a lease. There are many different items in a lease which can either save you or cost you depending on the approach you take.

THE START OF THE LEASE

Pick a day when the rent starts and stick to it. Most prospective tenants will need time to move out of their current unit and will try to tie up the property for a long time (thirty days) without payment. If they want it badly enough they will go along with one or two weeks of double rent.

Most new tenants want to start at the beginning of the month. Assenting to this can be used as a trade-off for other concessions the tenant wants which you don't want to give.

Assume he wants a new security door-chain to replace the one that is not in perfect shape. A single explanation of, "If you were to move in now and I had the rent for this month, I would be able to pick up a new chain for you, but with you waiting until the first to move in, I am losing three weeks' worth of rent."

THE SECURITY DEPOSIT

As I mentioned in chapter 10, there are two types of security deposits allowed in most states: refundable, which is always allowed, and nonrefundable, which is banned in a few states. Check your state laws to see if you are allowed to collect a nonrefundable deposit. The actual amount to be collected is a negotiable item, but don't bend too far. Check out what the other landlords are getting in your neighborhood, since you do want to be competitive, but be sure to protect yourself. If you are supplying furniture, the deposit should be higher. If there is a TV, you need to bargain for more.

A deposit for a pet is always a touchy topic. Many landlords do not allow pets at all; some charge a hefty deposit for pets. Some make pet deposits refundable and some make them non-refundable. Here's an idea, not used by many, but logically it should be since it is the best solution. Don't charge a deposit for a pet but negotiate a higher rent rate. Treat the pet as an extra person. They do use the apartment and they do consume the air conditioning and the heat. They wear out the carpet just as much as any tenant (if not more) and they do ruin the lawn and dirty the walk.

You will be surprised to see how many people will pay $15 or $20 more per month for a pet. Now you don't have the problem of returning a deposit. After five months you have covered a $100 deposit without having to give it back and all subsequent months are pure profit; also, you have increased the value of the building because you have increased its net operating income.

The Term of the Lease

As stated earlier, I do not believe in leases for residential tenants, either apartments or single-family homes. Judges won't uphold them anyway. This makes a lease a one-sided contract; you can't raise the rent, but the tenant can move out and break the lease at any time.

If you don't feel comfortable with a month-to-month agreement and you want a lease, then make sure it doesn't run out at the wrong time.

If you are a property owner near a university, structure your leases on a twelve-month cycle, not nine or ten, where you will sit empty during the summer, along with your fellow landlords.

I knew an investor in Michigan who owned many student units at the University of Michigan. Every May his vacancy rate went from zero to 40 percent. Like the other landlords he was always in trouble during the summer.

To compensate for possible lost rent, he took the total he needed over twelve months (example: $250 × 12 = $3,000) and divided it by ten months ($300) for a ten-month lease. This way he didn't care if the building sat empty for two months; he had all of his money. To make it easier to get tenants in the fall and to appear as a great landlord, he allowed any tenant with a ten-month lease ending in June to leave all of his or her belongings in the apartment for $20 per month during July and August, provided they sign a new ten-month lease that started in September. This appeared to be such a great deal, the apartments were handed down from one tenant to the next just to get the FREE two months.

Likewise, if you are in a resort area, don't let the lease run out at the end of the season. For example, May is the end of the tourist season in Scottsdale, Arizona; September in Cheyenne, Wyoming; and April is the last month for the ski resorts in the northeast and places like Vail and Aspen, Colorado.

Beware of the sharp and tricky lessee who signs a long-term lease and then leaves after the season or places a clause in the lease that lets him back out at the season's end.

One gentleman from Iowa, who shall be nameless, rented a condominium in Scottsdale at $1,200 per month. He put a clause in the lease stating that he could get out of the lease if he had medical problems and had to return to Iowa for treatment. At first the owners wouldn't go along with it, but when it was explained that the man had a heart condition, they agreed.

At the end of March, the end of the prime rental season, the owners received a letter from the tenant's doctor saying that his foot was infected and needed treatment. He used this as an escape clause to get out of the lease. He had no intention of staying six months. I'm sure he uses the same gimmick each year on some other unsuspecting owner or manager.

To avoid losing money on tenants like this one, we developed a new system for seasonal rentals. When negotiating a six-month lease during the prime season, we charge the same rent for the six-month period, but we collect it all in the first four months. If we charge $1,200 per month or $7,200 over six months, the lease reads $1,800 per month for January, February, March, and April, and $1 for May and June. Thus we get our money earlier and we aren't bothered by skips at the end of the season. If they walk out, there is no problem, and I may have a chance to rent the unit for the two remaining months.

Negotiating Utilities With the Tenant

In many buildings there is a central utility system, and, as an owner, you don't have much choice as to who pays the utilities. You are stuck with them unless you elect to spend a great deal of money putting the central system on computer so that you can meter percentages of usage by each apartment and bill each tenant.

The alternative to this is to have separate meters. When you are fortunate enough to purchase a building with separate meters you have the option of how to charge.

There are two schools of thought concerning charging. By having the tenants pay their own utilities, you eliminate the possibility of cost overruns and the possibility of a tenant's skipping out and still owing you on a utility bill. It is bad enough to lose rents, but you don't want to get stuck with a utility bill also.

However, if you give tenants a choice of either paying their own or having utilities included in the rent, you can make a great deal of money.

Many tenants want to negotiate a flat-rate rental because they are earning a regular salary and a flat rate is easier to budget for. This tenant does not mind paying extra as long as the amount is fixed. In such cases, negotiate a rate higher than the average monthly bill to give you a hedge in case of increases by the utility company.

If you are renting at the beginning of or during the high-utility season, adjust your rent schedule to be much higher during the first six months and then lower the rent during the off-season. Tenants will often rent with utilities paid during the high-utility season and then move out and into another complex where the rent is lower and pay their own utilities during the lower-utility season.

Prenegotiate the Move Out

One of the major conflicts between tenant and landlord is the money to be paid back when the tenant moves out. This conflict can be eliminated if you negotiate the move out at the time your new tenant moves in.

Go over with each new tenant exactly what you expect. Explain what you are going to charge for any damages or excessive cleaning needed. Give out a list explaining the charges (dirty refrigerators, $15, etc.). Now there can be no argument. Be fair, because an unhappy tenant at move-out time can be a real nuisance to you. If you are one of those landlords who keeps deposits unjustly, the word will spread rapidly and current tenants will say, "What the hell, we're not going to get our money back anyway so why bother to clean up?" Conversely, if you are honest and return deposits whenever possible, this word will spread and you will find your tenants going out of their way to return your unit to you in great condition. You will come out ahead financially by being a reputable landlord.

Collecting Rent

You will also have to be a tough, but fair landlord, because collecting rent is not always the easiest thing to do. When it comes time to collect rent, be firm. Set your limits and stick to them. I give the tenants a three-day leeway and then I start eviction proceedings. This is one area where negotiations do not help. For some reason many tenants feel their car and TV payments are more important than their rent. Perhaps they think that the bank will say, "Don't worry, Mr. Hoffman. You can be late on your payment since the tenants didn't pay their rent." The banks don't care. They want their money and this must be communicated to the tenant. By starting evictions on the fourth day after the rent is due the tenants will quickly learn that the time of rent payment is not negotiable, and it is due on the first day of the month. Tenants will have to find other money, instead of their rent, to fix their cars or make their loan payments. The moment you give in to one tenant, the word will spread that you are an easy mark.

Also, if a unit needs repairs, take care of it immediately so that the tenants will not be tempted to refuse to pay their rent until the repairs are done.

Rent Raises

Rent raises are negotiable and should be done on an independent basis. Each apartment is different either by location, view, size, age, or other factors.

A current tenant should not be paying the same amount as a new tenant moving in. The new tenant should pay more since you will not be able to raise his rent in the near future, while the old tenant can be given a rent raise when his lease comes up for renewal.

If you have a good tenant that you want to keep, make your raise lower than if you didn't care if he stayed or moved. If the market is soft but you expect the vacancy rate to be lower in the future, do a split raise. Let the tenants have a very small raise ($5 per unit) for the first six months, but after this period increase the rent $25 per unit to cover the next six months.

Checking for Damage

Negotiations even play a role in the actual move-out by a tenant. The diplomacy and tact you use can make or break both your cash flow and your reputation around the complex.

As I have mentioned, I am a fair but tough landlord and this applies to this facet of the operation as well. In my earlier days in this business I was very lenient and many times I would inspect an apartment for damage the night the tenant was moving out. This was "fair" to the tenant because he could walk with me and discuss the charges. It didn't take long for me to realize that his presence was not helpful.

I remember inspecting an apartment I owned in Michigan. Anything I found wrong with the apartment was either there when the tenant moved in (even though he forgot to put it on his check-in sheet) or was caused by mother nature or the manager or the neighbor, who should be billed, or was normal wear and tear that he shouldn't be charged for. After all was said and done I decided not to change my mind and I charged him for all the damage. He spent his last night in the complex telling all his friends what a rip-off artist I was. It did not make for good landlord-tenant relations.

Now I check the laws in each individual state and find out how many days I have to mail back the deposit check. I inform the tenants I will be checking out the apartment sometime during that period and will mail out the check and a list of any damages found during that period. Should there be any questions, they may question me after they have received their report. That way I am also covered for any damage done during farewell parties or the actual move-out.

Don't feel sorry for a tenant when you hear, "I'm moving out of state so I need my money now," or "I need the deposit back to give to a new landlord as a deposit." Life is tough for all of us and there are rules. Stick to yours.

After you have done your inspection, mail the check promptly. If you are making deductions, spell out the cause and the amount clearly. Make sure the check and list goes out within the designated time. By law, a late check could result in your not being allowed to take any deductions and possibly a penalty of up to three times the amount of the deposit you held.

If you don't have a forwarding address for a tenant, mail your list and check to the property address he rented. One of two things will happen. He will either have left a forwarding address with the postman and the letter will be forwarded or it will be returned to you with "no forwarding address left." If you get it back don't open the envelope. Just file it away sealed, with your check in it. This way, if the tenant ever takes you to court claiming you didn't return the deposit, you will have the sealed envelope with the postmark for the judge to open and present to the tenant.

Refine Your Negotiating Skills

What does it mean to be an effective negotiator? To have a successful sale? A completed deal? Good price and terms? Your negotiations do not begin or end with a signed contract. Whenever you exchange ideas with others under the intent to reach an agreement, you are negotiating. An effective negotiator recognizes opportunities to profit in every avenue of life, and utilizes his knowledge and skills to negotiate for a piece of the profit.

Negotiating With Utility Companies

Carol, a client of mine, once had to deal with a utility company over an enormous deposit required as security before she could transfer the utilities on a multi-unit apartment building she had recently purchased. She had paid two prior deposits to the company and did not see why an additional deposit would be necessary.

She could post a bond for the amount, but bonds are costly and issued by few companies. I suggested she contact the utility company directly, and in person. A face-to-face meeting carries more clout than a telephone call. Carol explained the situation, emphasizing the fact that she was a property owner and had already paid deposits on her other two buildings. In the end the billing officer didn't eliminate the deposit but reduced the amount significantly. Many local offices have the right to change the base-rate figures and Carol used her tact and negotiation skills to get a better deal.

If you have a similar problem but this technique doesn't work, ask to talk to the supervisor. They usually have more power to negotiate.

As a last resort, get the utility company to agree to take an assignment of a bank account and then place the money in a high-interest bank account with the interest payable to you.

Any way you do it, make sure you get an agreement stating just how long you will have to leave your funds deposited before you will get a release.

Insurance Agents

As in any other field, there are good and bad insurance agents. First, it's necessary to find a good agent and then to negotiate the best deal.

You are buying an insurance policy on a piece of property, so don't make the mistake of relying on a life insurance agent to do the right job for you. Even if you have a good friend who sells life insurance, don't use him. Get yourself an independent insurance agent who specializes in property and casualty. He will be able to value your property correctly and get you the best prices. Different insurance companies (including some of the large and better-known ones) become very competitive at various times. When they do, they reduce their rates to attract business. And they usually save money on the agent's commission. Often, with these cut-rate packages, the agent's share is so little that he doesn't want to place your business with that company. It is your job to convince the agent of your desire to use him for all of your business, as long as he looks out for your best interest.

Let Your Neighbor Increase Your Cash Flow

If you are just starting out in real estate, your first investment will probably be a small one: a single-family home, a small apartment complex, or an office building. As in other areas of business, the little guy always takes it on the nose. You can't afford your own maintenance crew, so you have to pay by the hour at a much higher rate.

All this can change if you use your imagination. If you need your lawn cared for, don't look in the Yellow Pages, look in your neighborhood. Other landlords have people doing their lawns. Either they are contracted or they are on-site managers. The point is that they are already there and they have the tools. Approach them with the concept of, "Since you're already doing Mr. Smith's lawn twice a month, and you have hauled the equipment out here, it will only take an additional thirty minutes each time to also do my lawn. If I give you an extra $20 it should more than handle the time put in."

During your conversation, make sure you let him know you won't let Mr. Smith know how good a deal you have. It will be a private agreement.

If you want to hire experienced maintenance or cleaning people for your apartments, and the units do not merit a resident manager, then approach the manager of the property nearby and offer him minimum wage or a little higher. He will likely be willing to keep an eye on your place and do a little maintenance when necessary. On-site resident managers receive so little compensation they are always grateful for extra income, but you must consider this: You must make it clear that you will never ask these people to do anything that will conflict with their jobs as managers for someone else. They will not be expected to find tenants for your building or work for you when they have work to do at their own complex. Explain that you know you come second.

However, the agreement will be a private affair between the two of you. Many times you and your neighbors will have different types of units. You may have furnished two-bedroom units, while your neighbor has studio or one-bedroom units vacant. So the manager you hire could suggest your units to someone looking for a two-bedroom apartment when he doesn't have a similar unit available.

Build a rapport with your neighbors and you may be able to swap potential tenants. If this doesn't work, go to their on-site managers and offer a finder's fee for sending you tenants. An extra $25 can be very attractive. Once again, make sure they understand you are only looking for their overflow; those prospects that don't rent from them for some reason. You are not trying to steal tenants.

Discount Purchases and How to Get Them

By now you know that you can increase the value of your property by increasing income or decreasing expenses. Getting discounts on your purchases is one way you can lower your expenses considerably.

Here are some tips on how to get discounts on buying products for your properties, whether it be paint, furniture, or anything in between.

1. Start a management company of your own even if you only have one property. Have business cards and checkbook printed with the company name, with you as President. Introduce yourself to the owner of the hardware store, used furniture shop, etc., as the new President of the company (don't let on that it is a new company) and let him know you are trying to make

cost-effective changes in the company and therefore you are looking to change your current suppliers. Then ask for a discount. If he wants to see volume first before discussing the discount turn the idea around and ask for the discount on a trial basis (sixty days) and you will be happy to review the volume after that time, either up or down. During the conversation, make sure you work in the list of people that will be authorized to sign for purchases by saying, "These will be the only ones allowed to sign for merchandise." If your company is a one-man show, list a few friends and neighbors. When you open a new checking account make sure you start your checks with a four-digit number so it will not look like you are starting a new account.

2. Contact a friend who is a decorator or contractor and ask if you can "work for him" and get cards printed. Most decorators and contractors get discounts from suppliers.

3. Take the role of the little employee in your company and after shopping in a particular store a few times (make yourself noticed each time by saying hello), ask to see the boss or manager. Let him know that you do your personal shopping here but your company does business with his competition. Say that you think his store is nicer although a little bit out of the way for the company. Ask for a credit application for your "boss" and suggest a small company discount might help to sway your "boss." That way it seems like the two of you are "plotting" to get the business. Everyone likes to have the edge.

Repairs and Improvements

As an owner, you will have to make repairs and do improvements to your property. The I.R.S. looks upon this in two ways. If you are doing maintenance or fixing something, you are allowed to deduct the cost of fixing as an expense to offset your income in the year the work is done. However, if you make a major improvement like putting on a new roof, then you have improved the value of the property and you may not deduct the improvement as an expense. You must depreciate the cost of the improvement over the life of the improvement. The latter can lead to a very bad cash flow and tax problem each year. The confusion arises when we have to define maintenance versus capital improvement. We would all agree that if you had a one-hundred shingle roof and one shingle needed repair, replacing it would be considered a repair. On the other hand, if all the shingles needed to be replaced, we would have a depreciable improvement. But what if only fifty shingles needed to be replaced? Would we have a repair or an improvement? I don't have the answer because I don't think the I.R.S. has the answer. It lies with how they interpret your return if you are audited. If you repair a burn hole in a carpet with a one-inch-by-one-inch patch we know it's a repair, but what happens if we repair a burn hole with a twelve-foot-by-twelve-foot patch, and the room is twelve feet by twelve feet? If there is a reasonable doubt about an expenditure, then have your accountant deduct it as an expense. The worst that will happen is that the I.R.S. will disallow it and you will have to pay what you would have had to pay anyway. On top of that, the I.R.S. has been known to negotiate or trade off one item for another.

Here are some hints:

1. It is always better to fix something than to replace it. For tax purposes it is better to spend $150.00 fixing an old refrigerator than it is to spend $150.00 on new "used" furniture.

2. If you need to fix something and it is near year-end and it is a major job that could be considered an improvement, do half the job in December and the other half in January.

3. Work with repairmen and contractors who will give you itemized receipts showing you "fixed," "repaired," or "corrected" items. Stay away from having things "replaced" or "installed."

Negotiating on Improvements

If you are going to make improvements on your property, the first decision is whether to do it yourself or not. Is this an item to negotiate? Sure it is! Negotiating with yourself is just as important as negotiating with other people.

You must decide whether the job is worth doing yourself. You can't deduct your labor as an expense and you could end up being penny-wise and pound foolish.

When I first started in real estate, my wife and I took three weekends to paint an apartment. We saved $150.00 in labor, but cost ourselves $300.00 in lost rent during that time. Was it worth it? Of course not, and we could have spent the three weeks looking for more property.

You also have to determine whether your marriage will be in jeopardy if you do the work yourself. I have heard many horror stories about husbands and wives doing repair and redecorating together. I know for a fact that my wife and I will never hang wallpaper together again. The last time we did, we didn't talk for days. It wasn't worth it. And the philosophy of doing it yourself to get it done properly the first time may work for many of you, but for me, it's a myth.

Look into all the tax benefits of hiring your children to do some of the work. Often times your spouse and children can work for you and save you many tax dollars. (You may want to listen to Joe Land's taped tax course, which has helped me save thousands of dollars in this and other tax areas.)

Fixed Bids *Versus* Other Methods

There are two different types of work to be done to a property, repair or improvement. The work can be major or minor.

If it is minor, I use firemen to do the work. At $5.50 or $6.00 an hour you get great service and by calling the local firehouse you can find "experts" in every field from landscaping to plumbing.

When it comes to major work we are talking about a whole new ballgame. The most important rule when dealing with contractors is get a "firm bid." There are many ways to hire contractors and all but the "firm bid" are wrong. If you are planning to do major work on a property, do not deal with a contractor on a "time and material" basis, where the contractor will do the work for the cost of the materials plus his time, or on a "cost plus" method, where the contractor will do the work and tack on 10 or 15 percent to the price of the job as his profit. Both of these methods leave no room for negotiation and open the door to possible cost overruns. When you are contracting a job, make sure you know the full cost before you start. The bid you receive should be complete right down to the last nail. You must ask for a written bid on the job and it must be in detail.

Contractors will tell you that if you request a firm written bid the total cost will be higher than if you use one of the other methods. This may be true in some cases, but with a written bid at least you have a complete bid before you start. This allows you to plan. If you are going to use this method, your ability to negotiate will play an important part in getting the right deal.

To get the best deal, request bids from several contractors. Ask the contractor to give you his best first bid, including any cost for contingencies. Then do the same with three or four other contractors. When all the bids are in, throw out the highest bid, because you are getting ripped off, and throw out the lowest bid, because that contractor will probably find a way to rip you off. Then look at the other bids. Meet with the contractors, go over their bids, and then negotiate by playing one against the other until you get the price you want. All of the negotiation techniques taught in this book apply to this type of negotiation.

C.Y.A.—Cover Your Assets

Don't overlook the hidden problems when you begin to negotiate. One slip at the wrong time and you'll see all your profits go down the drain.

Here are some safety tips:

1. *When negotiating with contractors, make sure they are bonded.* It will probably cost you more to have a bonded contractor, but the cost will be well worth it. This bond protects you against the contractor's walking out on the job and leaving you holding a bag of nails with a job half done.

If you don't want to pay for a bond in your bid, there are two ways to get around the cost. When you ask for a bid, make sure the contractors include the cost of a bond. Let them think you are going to require one. This will eliminate the ones who can't be bonded, because they won't waste their time on the bid. After you have the bid, tell the winning bidder you don't want the bond and have him reduce the price of the contract by the cost of the bond.

Your second alternative is to make sure the contract calls for you to hold back 10 percent of the job payment until ninety days after it is finished. By holding back on the payment you will always be ahead of the contractor in the event he does walk out.

2. *Make sure you get lien waivers from all workers and paid invoices for all materials.* Every time you have work done on your property you are putting yourself into double jeopardy. You are not only responsible to the contractor you employed,

but to each subcontractor and supplier as well, even though they are hired by the contractor.

It may not seem fair, but consider this scenario. If you hire a contractor to rebuild your kitchen and the contractor subcontracts a painter and carpenter to do the work, and if after you pay the contractor, he fails to pay his subcontractors, you are required to pay both of them.

Each state has different laws to protect you. Check with your attorney or the local agencies as to the amount of time you are liable for and how much notice each subcontractor must give you. However, there is one thing you can do in every state. Get lien waivers. Before you pay any contractor insist on signed waivers from each person on the job and demand paid invoices for all material used. The time to make these demands is when you are negotiating the contract. You are not insulting the contractor. He does business this way every day. In fact he probably keeps a pad of waivers in the glove compartment of his truck.

3. *Penalties and bonuses.* When dealing with many contractors, there is always the problem of time. For any number of reasons, many jobs just never seem to get done on time and often you are left with a tenant ready to move in and no place for him to move into.

To correct this situation, you should negotiate a penalty into the contract for each day the contractor is late. This doesn't guarantee the job will be done on time, but it will compensate for any days lost. If you are going to enter an agreement with a tenant for a specific day and you are relying on the contractor to finish the job on a specific date, make sure you put into the lease or rental agreement a clause which allows you to deliver the apartment late in case it is not finished in time. Without it, you could be facing a large loss in court to a very unhappy tenant.

To speed up the work, you might consider negotiating a bonus for getting the job done early.

4. *Worker's Compensation.* Another major item to be negotiated in any contract is Worker's Compensation. If your contractor doesn't cover his subcontractors and employees with Worker's Compensation and there is an injury on the job, you are going to be liable. Make sure you verify and insist on a policy.

Negotiating With Other
People

There is more to negotiating than just doing battle with the seller. Many other people are involved in a real estate transaction: the real estate agent, attorney, escrow officer, appraiser, and lenders.

How you handle each of these people will greatly affect the success of your transactions.

The Real Estate Agent

You will remember the story of "Pedro and the Bandido" and how easy it is to end up with a Pedro. This can be prevented if you are aware of certain facts.

There are three sides to every real estate transaction: the buyer's side, the seller's side, and the agent's side.

The agent's objective is to consummate a sale. Commissions are his lifeline. Without a contract there is no commission. In general, he doesn't care whether the buyer increases his offer or the seller decreases the selling price. If he can bring the two people together he has a sale, and that means a commission.

Most state laws require that all real estate agents involved in a transaction have a fiduciary responsibility to the person paying them, and since most contracts call for the seller to pay the commission, their allegiance is to the seller. Don't accept this as gospel. If you don't purchase the property, the seller doesn't have the money to pay the commissions, so in reality, it is you who are paying the agent.

How do you get fair representation? There are many ways. Let's discuss the two easiest methods.

First, never call an agent who has a listing in the newspaper. He has an exclusive listing from the seller and he will be looking out for the seller's interests. If you see an ad or ads in the paper that attract you and you wish to pursue them, then get your own agent, one you can trust and talk to about the properties. He will contact the listing agent and get the facts for you.

For representing you, your agent will receive one-half of the listing agent's commission. To prevent any conflict, it is advisable to have the listing agent deliver a note from you to the seller notifying him of your intention to use your own agent for the transaction.

A second way to get better representation from your agent is to enter into a "buyer's broker" agreement. This agreement simply states that you are willing to pay the agent a fee (flat or percentage) to select properties and negotiate all offers with you.

This gives him an exclusive right to represent you. Of course, you are committed to him for a period of time on any purchase you make. There are both pros and cons to having a buyer's broker agreement. On the one hand, if you have picked a good agent, he knows he will receive a commission when you buy and he will work much harder for you. On the other hand, you are committed to one agent and you cannot have various agents working for you.

Under the buyer's broker agreement, the broker does not get paid by the seller but by you. Therefore he will generally work to negotiate lower prices on your purchases.

The Attorney

In many states attorneys are not used in real estate transactions. Both buyer and seller simply rely on title and escrow companies to do all of the legal work necessary to close the deal. This is a mistake.

Regardless of what is normal practice in your state, you should have an attorney. He is the only one who is truly your representative. You pay him to represent you and look out for your interests. A title company represents only itself and is only required to correct the paperwork between buyer and seller in order to process a legal transaction.

Choosing a good attorney can be a problem. Since attorneys do not advertise a specialty such as divorce, accidents, corporate law, or real estate law, it is up to you to select and negotiate for a good attorney. Don't use a particular attorney because he did a great job in handling your divorce. He may be outstanding in the courtroom, but limited in his knowledge of real estate law. Again, you pay him as you would any other employee and therefore you deserve to choose one you feel is appropriate.

Once you decide you are talking to a knowledgeable attorney, the next problem is cost. Many charge 1 percent of every purchase price. I will not work with these attorneys. The lawyer doesn't do any more work on a $100,000 home than he does on a $50,000 home, so why should he be paid twice as much? Either agree to a flat rate up front or to an hourly rate if a transaction becomes quite complex. If you do agree on an hourly rate, get a written estimate and insist that you be kept informed at various levels so you won't be surprised at the end. Find out the rates for his time and also for his clerks and secretary. Then you should negotiate your agreement so that you pay a different rate for each service his office provides for you, depending on who does the work.

Don't use an attorney unnecessarily. There will be many houses and investment properties you will offer on and never come to terms on with the seller. If you pay an attorney to read each contract before you present it, all of your profits will be spent on legal fees.

Do your homework. Write your offers. Negotiate the contract, and make sure you have included a weasel clause in each one. When you have completed the negotiations, checked the books, records, leases, and physical property, and you are satisfied, *then* have the attorney read the contract. If it needs to be changed, don't remove contingencies until after you have negotiated the changes.

I have drastically reduced the fees for my syndications because I utilize my office word processor to develop the necessary prospectus and agreements. Instead of paying the going rate of between $6,000 and $7,000, I pay $2,500, which covers the time spent by the attorney to review, correct, and update the memorandum and agreements, but the actual physical corrections and typing are done by my secretary.

If you are working on a transaction that is speculative, and could fall apart before closing, then look for an attorney who will work on a contingency basis. If the deal goes through, he receives more than his normal rate; however, should it fail, he will receive no compensation. There are many attorneys willing to work on this basis after reviewing the transaction and making a value judgment on the success of the venture.

There are also many lawyers who will work on an equity participation basis, where they receive part ownership in lieu of cash. This is a very popular method of payment in partnerships and syndications. You are provided with ongoing legal advice from one of the partners who also holds a personal interest in the profitability of the investment.

When selecting an attorney, interview three or four candidates before making your final decision. It's your money, so be careful, but don't base your decision on money only. You will have to rely on your attorney's integrity and knowledge of the law. What you stand to lose may be far greater than his fees.

The Title or Escrow Company

In all states, there are title companies that will issue a title policy insuring that the buyer gets a clear title to the property. Many states use this method of transfer exclusively, while others still use the method of actually having the "abstract of title" pass from seller to buyer and they rely on the buyer's attorney to give an opinion on the transfer of the title to the buyer. Likewise, some states have escrow companies established to handle the legal transfers of title, while others rely strictly on real estate companies and attorneys to close the deal. Finally, some states combine title and escrow companies for real estate transactions.

The rates charged by title and escrow companies are often regulated by the state. With fixed rates it would seem that there is very little room to negotiate. This is not true. If you are buying a house to live in and plan on spending the next ten years there then just pick a large, reliable title or escrow company to handle the purchase. However, if you are starting to buy properties for investment and plan to make many transactions, then it is critical to select a company that meets your requirements. I have found it is not the company that is important, but the individual escrow officer who makes the difference.

What are some guidelines in choosing a good escrow/title company? First, choose a company where the escrow officers get paid a commission, as opposed to a straight salary. You will get much better service if the officer is rewarded with respect and referral business.

Next, check the rates. Some companies give discounts to builders, while others allow you to purchase a binder instead of a policy. To do this you might have to pay a premium of 10 to

25 percent of the policy, but should you sell the property within from six to eighteen months you will be able to provide a policy to the new purchaser free, with the exception of the increased amount of coverage.

Most companies charge for a preliminary title report, which shows who owns the property and whether there are any liens against it. This is generally waived if the transaction is completed, but the person who orders the report must pay for it if the deal falls through.

Work with one company and give them your business. If you negotiate well, you will be able to get the preliminary title report free and will also be able to convince them to give you lists of comparable sales in the areas of your purchases. This will come in handy when selecting potential properties to write offers on.

The Appraiser

If you are applying for a bank loan or a loan from any financial institution you will probably need an appraisal. The appraiser gathers as much information as he can on your property and on the properties in the area. Based on this information, and information from previous appraisals, current sales, and the appraiser's personal prejudices and convictions, he will assign a value to the property.

If he is working for a lending institution his appraisal will most likely be for an amount less than the value placed on it by the real estate agent. The agent values the property high to get the listing, and the appraiser values it low to protect his client's equity position.

Appraisers are human beings; they have good days and bad days. They catch colds, stay up late at night, and worry about financial problems. It is important that you realize that an appraiser's valuations can be affected by his moods. A $100,000 home today could be worth $105,000 tomorrow or $95,000 a week from now.

But overall, appraisers are honest people. Generally they cannot be bribed or bought and I don't advocate doing anything of the kind. However, anytime you are dealing with human nature you can influence a decision by taking certain actions. Try this the next time you get an appraisal:

Meet with the appraiser. Give him the facts and figures you have. Let him know how you valued the property. Go over the comparables you used to make your analysis. If he can save work because you have done it for him, he will probably use your numbers.

If you have a contract on the property, let him see it. If you have made a personal contract he will try his best to help make the deal work. Use tact to get your way because you certainly don't want to antagonize him.

The Financiers

As children we learned that "a penny saved is a penny earned" and we should all save money for a "rainy day." When the time came to borrow money, we were told our "friendly banker" was right there to help us.

The only trouble with getting help from the bank is that we have to prove to the banker that we don't need the money in order to get it.

Dealing with lenders can be intimidating, but you must get over the fear of dealing with a banker. He is simply a businessman in the business of lending money. If he doesn't lend money, then the bank cannot show a profit and will suffer a loss. You see, the bank must pay interest to their depositors as well as cover the costs of advertising, salaries, rents, and other expenses. The interest earned on monies loaned is a bank's major source of income to cover these costs.

Banks want to lend you money, but at the same time, they have a responsibility to their investors and depositors. The loans they make are done so with the expectation that they will be repaid. Lenders do not want the collateral you put up to obtain the loan. They are not in the business of selling real estate, cars, or furniture. Instead they prefer to be repaid on time. The taking of collateral is security to protect the loan in the event of default. In reality, lenders want to earn interest and have the loan repaid in full so they can lend the funds out to someone else.

So why the tough image? Banks feel the firm impression they portray will convince you to pay on time and conform to their rules. In actual fact, you can do a lot of negotiating with banks and other institutions. Interest rates not only vary from one bank to the next, but will often vary within each bank depending upon the type of loan and the loan officer you speak with.

One Sunday, in Portland, Oregon, the local newspaper published the local rate for home mortgages at a few of the major banks. The rates for the same conventional loans varied from 13½ percent to 16½ percent. On a $100,000 loan the monthly payments differed by as much as $250 and the points required to start the loan differed by over $1,000.

Why the discrepancy? Some banks have more money to lend than others. If the bank has just purchased money from one of their many sources, then they have to get the money into the marketplace and will be much easeir to deal with.

Points

Like interest rates, points are very negotiable items. Lenders charge points (equal to 1 percent of the face value of the loan) for two reasons. First, to cover the bookkeeping and start-up costs associated with a new loan. Second, to compensate for making loans at a lower-than-normal interest rate.

Naturally, lenders will attempt to charge as many points as possible. The more points you pay, and the shorter the period of time the note is carried, the higher your effective interest rate will be. Let's say Mr. Mullins wanted to borrow $10,000. After speaking with the loan officer, he is given a choice between a one-year or five-year loan at 10 percent interest plus five points to cover processing charges. If he chooses the one-year note, his interest payment will be only $1,000 (10% × $10,000). However, when Mr. Mullins adds in the $500 he is charged for points (5% × $10,000), he discovers that his effective rate of interest will not be 10 percent but actually 15 percent. Furthermore, the $500 is paid up front so he really receives only $9,500.

Now if Mr. Mullins stretched the note to five years, a different scenario appears. The interest paid will be $5,000 over the five years plus the one-time fee of $500 at the beginning of the loan. If Mr. Mullins selected this option he would be paying a total of $5,500, or $1,100 per year, to borrow the $10,000. This works out to be 11 percent annual interest. The longer the loan, the less costly the point fee to process the loan. Needless to say, Mr. Mullins should choose the five-year plan.

The type of loan you choose as well as the repayment period are also very important issues to be negotiated. Before dealing with a moneylender become an expert in the various types of loans available. Determine if you would prefer low payments, graduated payment mortgages, interest-only, reverse capitalization, notes or the traditional higher payment amortized loan, where you build equity.

Whichever type of financing you choose, don't box yourself in with a balloon note that is due in a few years, unless you are prepared to pay it off or are certain you can arrange other financing.

When negotiating with a bank official don't hesitate to mention the number of accounts you have with the bank or what your annual flow-through is (referred to as "overnight"). Obviously it is better to keep your cash with the same bank as your loans, but it will not do any good unless the loan officer is aware of it. Blow your horn. Invite the local officer to lunch and be casual. Don't ask him for a loan, just get acquainted with each other. You are interviewing him to decide whether you want to do business with him.

If for some reason you do not get the terms you wanted, don't hesitate to use your power to influence and negotiate with a competing bank.

Four years ago, I was a very satisfied customer with a local bank in Phoenix. I had several checking and savings accounts, each with large deposits. For three years my track record with the bank went unblemished. As a new Phoenix resident, I had established an excellent credit rating and increased my ability to borrow. I applied for a $3,000 loan to purchase a car phone.

My checking accounts with the bank far exceeded the loan amount but I preferred to borrow the $3,000 in lieu of using my own cash. Therefore, I assumed there would be no problem.

Shortly after being greeted by a new branch manager, I presented my request and was told he would need to check my accounts and credit rating. Shortly after lunch that day, I was informed that since I had no credit history on file with the credit bureau (which was an error they caught later), the bank said it could not reach a decision until the next day. I explained to the gentleman that time was of the essence and that if the loan was not granted today, I would withdraw all accounts. Still he held to his "no decision until tomorrow" commitment. At two o'clock sharp I walked into another bank, discussed my situation with the senior officer, and in fifteen minutes was granted the loan. He made the loan based on my financial statements plus the information on the account I agreed to transfer to his bank. By four P.M. more than a million dollars a year in deposits was transferred from the first bank to the second. Quite a price to pay for a $3,000 loan.

Don't be afraid to use your assets to negotiate with bankers.

That is the language they understand. If you can help them make a profit, they will do the same for you.

"Due-on-sale" and "acceleration" clauses are a final important element of your financial negotiations. Many savings and loans and banks are attempting to rid themselves of their low-interest-bearing loans made during the 1960s and 1970s. With the support of the 1982 Supreme Court ruling, many lenders are enforcing paragraph 17 of their contracts to all the notes due on any properties where the title transfers ownership. To sidestep this situation, investors have developed enough schemes to fill a library. I will address the area of negotiating with the bank when you don't use these other methods.   _ FNMA

First, have the bank check to make sure they haven't sold the loan to one of the many agencies that buy loans. If they have, their right to accelerate is gone. However, they will not give out this information unless you ask for it.

If the loan is one they can accelerate, keep in mind that they would prefer not to call in the loan or forfeit you out of the property. Their goal is to raise the interest rate to a more attractive level to cover the cost of the money they borrow. Bankers are business men and if you can show that a building you are purchasing will not support a higher interest rate, then you can often negotiate a compromise in the form of a blend note or blend loan. If you are attempting to obtain a blend loan then your numbers in support of your request must be accurate and your entire proposal must be well planned. The more information you can give to support your position, the greater the likelihood to negotiate a lower rate. Bankers want to be fair. You just have to show them what fair means to you.

Marketing Your Property

Until now we have discussed how you can negotiate and fix up property as a buyer. Now it's time to look at what you do when you're ready to sell your building. You could just buy properties and live off of their cash flows. But to make the most money in the shortest amount of time you'll have to sell your properties for a profit.

Make Them Want to Buy

You can make ANY property easy to sell. To do so you must be able to reach the greatest number of potential buyers. You accomplish this by:

1. Being able to offer your property for little or nothing down.
2. Offering the property with no loan-qualifying requirements.

Think about it. If you were a typical buyer you would want to buy with little or no down payment. As a seller you want to sell for all cash in order to get all of your equity out of the building. There is nothing wrong with this philosophy, but it may not work to your advantage. Trying to sell your property for a large cash-down payment will eliminate most of your buyers.

Remember the old adage, "If you get a good price, you have

to give in to better terms. If you get great terms, you have to give up on price." If the building you sell requires all cash or 50 percent down you will have to lower your price.

This doesn't mean you can't ever pull any cash out of the property. It is possible to sell your property for a premium price and still get a substantial down payment.

Let's say you have an apartment building for sale that's worth $100,000. The only loan on the property is for $27,000 and you need enough cash to buy another building. Since lenders will let you borrow up to 80 percent of the property's value, you decide to refinance the building for $80,000, pay off the $27,000 loan, and put the remainder into your pocket.

Now you can offer your building for 10 percent down, carryback 10 percent, and let the buyer assume the $80,000 loan you just took out. An attractive deal to any buyer.

You could go one step further by taking your carryback note and selling it in the second-mortgage market, a place where trust deeds and mortgages are traded daily. Of course you'll have to take a discount. The amount of that discount will depend upon your ability to negotiate and on the terms of the note created. A three-year note with amortized payments will certainly be more attractive than a seven-year interest-only note.

Be a Chameleon

Remember that when negotiating, the buyer and the seller will be diametrically opposed to one another on most issues of the contract. It's up to you to set your negotiating strategy and proceed in that direction. Thus to be a successful negotiator, you must be able to perform as a top-notch buyer when purchasing properties, then change your whole approach to negotiate as a seller when marketing the building.

As a seller you would be better off to refuse to carryback any note that is longer than three years. By doing so you open yourself up to the same problems the banks faced when they lent money out for thirty years at 8 and 9 percent while having to pay 11 and 12 percent to savings accounts. If you have to take a note with a term longer than three years, be sure to include an interest rate adjustment clause that reads, "Interest rate shall be two (2%) percent over the prime lending rate, adjusted every six months, with the first adjustment beginning three years from close of escrow." Also, make sure there is a due-on-sale clause requiring the buyer to pay off the note in the event he sells the property to a third party.

Other clauses to be included in your negotiations would be a prepayment penalty, late payment charge, an "as is" clause, and an option clause in the event the escrow doesn't close. It would be to your benefit as a seller to include a rent-assignment clause to protect your position if the buyer doesn't make his mortgage payments. This clause allows you to collect the rents while you proceed with foreclosure. It also prevents the buyer from milking the building while in the process of losing it.

Obviously as a buyer you would oppose all of the aforementioned statements. Instead, you would fight tooth and nail for clauses such as exculpatory clauses, loan subordination, and nominating clauses.

In essence, you need to establish a set of negotiation guidelines for you as the buyer and a different set for you as the seller. Appendix A lists all of the major clauses from both the buyer's and seller's point of view.

A good negotiator will succeed regardless of the position he takes. He either gets his way or he finds another deal. A poor negotiator usually makes the bad deals and then wonders, "What went wrong with my investment?"

To List or Not to List

That is the question that puzzles every seller. "Why pay a real estate broker when I can sell the property myself?" you think. And there is no one right answer. You can elect to sell the building yourself and save anywhere from 5 to 7 percent of the selling price. However, if you choose this path, be prepared. Your agent does a lot more technical work than you may have thought. Before you eliminate the idea of using a broker take a look at some of the benefits of using a GOOD real estate agent.

1. Agents help you price your real estate at a level that is not too low, yet will sell in a reasonable period of time. Many times a full market analysis is included as part of their service.

2. Agents can do the early negotiations for you and eliminate people who aren't serious prospects and will waste your time.

3. Agents help you analyze any offers you receive and assist you in writing a counter-offer. Have you ever tried to write a contract yourself? Which contract do you use? Are you sure the paperwork is completed correctly? Many sellers feel safe to leave the paperwork to the escrow agent or title company, but they will do nothing but legalize the agreement between you and the buyer.

If you live in a state where investors rely on an attorney to help, then you had better find a good one. Many attorneys spend such a small portion of their time on real estate that they do not have the expertise to handle a real estate contract.

4. Agents can represent you and keep the negotiations on an even keel. The old saying, "He who has himself as an attorney, has a fool for a client," also holds true for real estate. Naturally your feelings will emerge when you negotiate. They are best

kept out of the deal. Unless you are a skilled negotiator you should have an experienced agent assist you.

5. The multiple listing service is something that makes a realtor valuable. He can list your property for every other realtor to see, and give it much more exposure to qualified buyers.

In all, until you are accustomed to negotiating as a principal, the money you spend on an agent's commissions could yield you a healthy return.

Sell or Exchange?

Another decision you will be faced with when you own a piece of property is whether you should sell it outright or exchange it for another property. The government makes it quite favorable to trade by allowing us to defer indefinitely any taxes on the gain on the sale. Through the use of a 1031 tax-deferred exchange you are given the opportunity to exchange your property for another and thus avoid paying taxes at that time.

In its simplest form, an exchange occurs when you trade your property for another's property. To qualify for a tax-deferred exchange you need to follow these legal guidelines:

1. The property you are exchanging and the property you are receiving must be "like for like." In other words, property held for investment must be exchanged for investment property.

2. Both properties must be real property. You cannot trade a piece of art for an apartment building and still receive tax-deferred benefits.

3. The new mortgage you will be paying must be greater than or equal to the mortgage you trade.

4. The equity in the building you receive must be greater than or equal to the equity in the building you trade.

5. You will be taxed when you eventually sell outright.

In addition you need to:

1. Find someone willing to trade his property for yours and reach an agreement on the value of both properties.

2. Make sure each party understands why it is advantageous to exchange his property for another one.

3. Find a competent real estate broker and an accountant, an attorney and/or escrow agent who know what it takes to do a 1031 tax-deferred exchange. It has been my experience that 95 percent of all exchanges never reach close of escrow because the people hired to do the technical work do not have the expertise.

It is crucial to have experienced people represent you in such deals. Get recommendations from other people or sit down with your proposed professional advisor and interview him. You are doing the hiring, so the professional should be willing to spend a little free time with you to go over his qualifications.

4. Finally, persuade the other party to go through with the exchange. If the person you are working with is accustomed only to selling his property and paying taxes it might be difficult to convince him otherwise.

A Sample Exchange

To clarify the exchange process let's go over a sample exchange. You are the proud owner of a single-family rental house which you purchased for $60,000 in 1982. Now the house is worth $80,000, you owe $30,000, and your equity is $50,000. You heard that a 1031 tax-deferred exchange could give you leverage, greater tax write-off, and an opportunity to defer the capital gains taxes.

If you choose to sell outright and buy another rental you will have to pay taxes on your long-term capital gain. Furthermore, if you used accelerated depreciation, the tax bite will be even greater because your tax basis will be so low.

So you decide to go through with an exchange. You find an owner of an eightplex with a value of $200,000. The mortgage on the property is $120,000 and his equity is $80,000. As a result you have the following situation:

Your House		Eightplex
$80,000	Market value	$200,000
− 30,000	Mortgage	− 120,000
$50,000	Equity	$80,000

Now is the point where your negotiating skills take over. You will have to negotiate an agreement on the value of both properties with the other party. Be realistic. Don't be tempted to value your property for more than it is worth and discount the other property below market value.

Once an agreement on property value has been reached you are ready to balance the equity. The owner of an eightplex with $80,000 in equity certainly won't trade it for your house with only $50,000 in equity. You will have to give him something else to make up the difference between your equity and his (roughly $30,000). You might throw in a 1957 Thunderbird or a $30,000 note you have from a prior transaction. Perhaps you have a piece of jewelry you could trade. The key is to trade as little as possible.

In an exchange don't be too concerned with the value of your property or of the property you are acquiring. The equity is important, but equity is just an arbitrary number that shows the difference between the amount owed and the market value of the property. Fair market value is what you as a negotiator can get for it in the present market, not what an appraiser says it is worth.

If you can negotiate an eightplex with a $120,000 mortgage in trade for your single-family rental and a 1957 Thunderbird, you may have made a pretty good deal. However, if you had to include the piece of jewelry then you didn't negotiate as well. On the other hand, if you traded the trust deed (with a face value of $30,000) and your single-family home for the eightplex, and kept the car and jewelry, you did a great job. The value of the exchange pivots on your ability to trade as little as possible for as much as possible.

Everything you give the other party other than real property is considered "boot." All boot is taxable to the person receiving it. Since the owner of the eightplex will receive other valuables in addition to your house, he will have a partial 1031 tax-deferred exchange and pay taxes on the boot. You, on the other hand, qualify for a fully deferred exchange.

Since the owner of the eightplex will receive a smaller mortgage than that which he is trading he has received "mortgage relief." Mortgage relief is also treated as "boot" and, as such, is taxable.

Other alternatives exist beyond the two-way exchange. Many exchanges involve three or more participants and can be quite complicated.

I have only given you an overview of the exchange process. Exchanges are often very involved. You'll need the assistance of competent professionals to help you through the exchange and to go over all of the advantages and disadvantages with you personally. (I recommend the works of Joe Land and Dan Santucci, both experts on the 1031 tax-deferred exchange.)

It's important to note that for any building you exchange that was purchased prior to January 1, 1981, you are obligated by law to carry over the old depreciation schedule to your new building. Thus, if you were depreciating a building you purchased in 1979 over a thirty-year period, upon trade you would have to use the same thirty-year depreciation on the new building you receive. To some investors it is better to sell their older buildings outright and buy another apartment in which they can utilize the faster depreciation schedules put into effect as of January 1, 1981.

What Is Important as the Seller?

The most important item right now is to get the deal closed. There is no point to negotiating a contract, listing a property, holding the inspection, and entering escrow, if no deal is made.

Be firm, but be flexible. A good deal can slip through your fingers if you are too rigid. The reason you are selling your building is to make a profit and move on to the next deal. That's the objective of the whole investment process.

All You Need Now Is
Chutzpah

The real estate investor who pursues each deal with a winning vitality is one for whom I feel a special affinity. He is a leader who intends to make investments a lifetime pursuit. Each deal he negotiates is, for him, another step down the path to financial independence. He considers himself part of a winning elite group and is determined to move up the ladder of success.

If you feel this way, most of what you have read in this book should become second nature to you. You have absorbed the philosophy and know-how of effective negotiating and hopefully are already putting a few of the techniques into practice.

Some of my suggestions, however, deserve emphasis, and to assist you in your real estate dealings, I want to review some and add a few more that will be valuable to you.

Ten Keys to Successful Negotiation

1. *All sellers are liars, all buyers are thieves.* When dealing with people professionally, trust is a word that should be left at home. All of us would like to trust and believe in our fellow man, but it just doesn't work that way all the time. In real estate, the best negotiators take an "all sellers are liars and all buyers are thieves" approach to their deals. Granted, many people are honest by nature, but in a real estate transaction a transformation often takes place. People are people, and we have to learn to live with their idiosyncracies.

During a real estate transaction, even the most devout, church-going, ethical seller can transform into a convincing liar. He may increase his rental schedule, omit expenses, falsify utility bills, and eliminate vacancies in order to increase the value of his property.

Sellers aren't alone; buyers are no better. They distort the national and local statistics on vacancy, or hide any recent neighborhood sales figures that may be bad for them and show only those that would lower the value of the property. They may lie about their available cash in order to put less down or try to negotiate right before the close of the deal when they know they have the seller at a disadvantage.

The best advice I can give to you when negotiating with sellers or buyers is to not believe anything you hear unless you have verified it. And then get it in writing. If it isn't in writing then it doesn't exist.

2. *You make money when you buy real estate; you realize your profit when you sell it.* It's a fact of life that no one is willing to pay more for a piece of property than it's worth. You may find a sucker once in a while who will overpay but they are few and far between. If your real estate career depends on finding these gullible individuals then I would suggest a new direction. In real estate, supply and demand play an important role. If you attempt to overprice your property, you will be left sitting on it until the market either catches your appraisal or you lower your price.

You see, when you are ready to sell, the selling price will be based on the fair market value. Therefore, the real place to make your profit is at the time of purchase. If you negotiate a piece of property down below fair market value at the time of purchase, you will have already made your money.

To do this, you must base your purchase price at least 10 percent below the market. If you can purchase at 10 percent below market value, you can still sell at market value, pay a commission and closing cost, and get out without a loss if you have too.

To be able to purchase at 10 percent below market, you must make an initial offer of at least 10 percent below your *final price.* To illustrate this, let's say you want to buy a building that's listed at $200,000. Since you only want to pay $180,000 for the property you would start your negotiation with an offer of $162,000 (10 percent less than $180,000). This will hopefully give you enough room to negotiate and ensure a successful acquisition at $180,000.

Do not base your offer on any anticipated future event. Often a seller will approach you with statements such as, "You can raise the rents as soon as you take over," or "If you can get the zoning changed, you will be able to double your money." My response for this is, "If it were that simple, the seller would have already taken the action."

One more point. Do not fall into the trap of bailing out the seller. So many times I have heard a buyer tell me that he put too much down because the seller needed it, or because that's what the seller had in the property. Whose team are you playing for? Two wrongs don't make a right. If you pay the seller what he wants he will be bailed out and you will inherit his problems. You'll want to determine which "hot button" meets his needs, but not if it means ruining the profit potential for you. Always base your offer, both price and terms, on what the property is worth.

3. *A contract is a debate with separate battles called clauses.*
Most people look at a contract as one document between a buyer and a seller. The contract is actually a series of paragraphs, each developed to benefit the seller or buyer. In the end, the entire contract is usually slanted to one side or the other.

Be prepared: These people you are negotiating with will be out to get whatever they can from you. It is as simple as that. They will want the best price, the highest interest, the shortest loan period, the largest earnest deposit, the shortest contingency period, the fastest closing, the largest late-payment penalty, and the best prepayment penalty. They will do whatever it takes to get these things. If it means increasing the true income or leaving out some of the expenses, the seller will do it. Hiding a leaky roof, neglecting to inform the buyer of a waterpipe problem, filling the units with friends to show a full occupancy, or giving away free rent as a move-in incentive are just a few of the tricks used by sellers.

If you go into a negotiation with the belief that the other party is a crafty negotiator, you will always come out ahead because you will stay on your toes. We all want to believe in the basic honesty of all people, including those we have business dealings with. I'm not asking you to change your philosophy, just to verify everything and assume nothing.

Accept nothing at face value. Every item must be challenged. Every lease must be read. Every utility bill checked. Develop some formulas to check the seller. By doing so you can eliminate some of the headaches that might arise after escrow closes.

Here are a few of the formulas and rules that have worked well for me:

1. Laundry income should be no more than $3 per unit per month.
2. Vacancy should be no less than 5 percent of gross income.
3. Maintenance should be no less than 5 percent of the gross income.
4. Count on a minimum of $10 per apartment unit per month for a property manager.
5. Allow 5 percent of gross rent for professional management even if you are going to manage it yourself.
6. Count the utility meters and make sure you see the last twelve bills for each meter.
7. Read each lease or rental agreement and have each tenant sign a statement of security deposit made, not-

ing whether there was any prepaid or free rent he feels he is entitled to.

8. Add in dollars for advertising, supplies, legal fees, and for reserve.

9. Read the titles policy word for word to avoid legal problems later.

10. Read the underlying encumbrances carefully and check for balloons, prepayment penalties, and due-on-sale clauses. Sellers often "forget" about little items such as these.

11. The total expenses should be 35–40 percent of the gross income if the tenants are paying the utilities and between 40 and 45 percent if the owner is paying the expenses.

4. *Never give in . . . trade off.* Any basic book on negotiation will tell you never to offer what you want to end up with. They suggest you simply start higher or lower and work your way toward the actual price, terms, time, and so on.

For the most part, this holds true for the novice negotiator. However, it can be like saying to a beginning tennis player, "Here is the racket, throw the ball up and hit it into the other court." Many times he will not hit it within bounds. Similarly, as a novice negotiator, you may not always make the deal. If you do, it may not have the best terms. When negotiating a real estate deal you need an edge—a negotiation technique to help you get the deal you want. One such technique is called the "Never give in . . . trade off" method. In short, this means that you always tie one compromise to another.

Let me illustrate this technique with some examples. Let's suppose you start with the idea that you would like to buy a fourplex for $100,000, with $10,000 down and an interest-only loan for the balance of $90,000 at 10 percent for seven years. On the other hand, the seller wants $110,000, $20,000 down, and 12 percent for three years. Following the basic principle mentioned earlier, you start your negotiations at $81,000, 8 percent for ten years with $5,000 down, realizing there will be a counter-offer.

The first response you receive from the seller is for $15,000 down, so you counter with $8,000. He changes to $12,000, you up yours to $9,000. He says $11,000 and you say $10,000. And he agrees. Sound all right? Wrong! Everything went right until you said $10,000. You should have said $9,500 and when he counters with, say, $10,000, you say "OK" and add "I'll go along with your $10,000 if you give me the ten years I want." Even though your original concept was to give $10,000 down, there is no need for the seller to know that. Let him think he has won. Continue on with this routine. As you negotiate the length of the loan, he may say five years. You, of course, counter with nine, while he asks for six years. You offer eight. He brings up seven, and again you agree, provided he'll concede to 8 percent interest-only. He counters at 11 percent, you offer 9 percent, and he comes down to 10 percent. You have now negotiated and achieved all three of your points; meanwhile, the seller feels he has won.

Obviously by using this method you most likely give up a piece of your pride, since your objective is to have the other side believe they suggested the compromise first. However, in the long run you achieve the goals you set out for, and your opponent feels satisfied that he got his way.

5. *My 99 percent rule.* When negotiating, remember to keep in mind that 99 percent of all people are sheep, and only 1 percent of the population are shepherds. Those who are willing to learn, to advance, and to take charge join this elite group of the 1 percent.

Being part of the 1 percent is not always a birthright. It is something you must learn. Unfortunately, it is often easier to be part of the 99 percent because we are trained from birth to join this majority.

Most people set limits on themselves that aren't there. They are so used to following that they never think of themselves as leaders.

If you take the initiative and act with confidence, you will win more times than not. Notice the referee or umpire at the next sporting event. When he makes a call, he says it loud and without hesitation. If he were to hesitate or show any sign of doubt, the other side would be out arguing with him. But because he plays a leadership role, most calls go uncontested, though many later prove to have been wrong.

To be successful in real estate, you need to be a leader. Take control of the negotiations. Go with your real estate agent when he presents your offer and include in the contract a clause that states you have the right to handle the negotiations, although you do not have to enforce this clause unless you feel the agent is not doing the best job. Let the agent know you do not intend to interfere unless negotiations break down. This will not only make him feel part of a team, but also encourage him to do a better job.

6. *Never use a standard or residential contract to buy income property.* Picture this situation: You have just agreed to submit an offer on an eight-unit apartment building. The real estate agent fills out the purchase contract according to the specifications of your offer and asks you to sign by the "X." As you start to read over the document he adds with an obvious note, "Don't worry, it's a standard contract. Our office uses them on all our deals." You look at the smile on his face and sign the contract so you won't look like an amateur.

Unfortunately the word "standard" is used for too many contracts. The only person it is standard for is the individual writing the contract, and the only points these contracts may have in common are:

1. They are designed for the purchase of residential property.
2. They are written to favor the seller.

If you should sign one of these legally binding contracts, you will discover that most of your negotiations will occur after you think you have reached an agreement with the other party. On many occasions, the standard contract doesn't begin to cover important issues such as security deposits, late payment penalties, subordination clauses, exchange clauses, contingency (or weasel) clauses, or options.

Know the contents before you sign. Better yet, use your own contract. Create a "standard contract" that includes any clause you deem desirable. Read other contracts that are presented to you and pick out the good clauses to put into yours. Soon you will have a contract to cover every conceivable problem. When you want to make an offer or counter-offer, just dig into your file of paragraphs and clauses and pull out the one you need for the occasion. This way all of your negotiations will be up front —not after the fact.

7. *Never negotiate with yourself.* After reading this book it's obvious that you wouldn't negotiate with yourself. Or would you? In fact, you may be doing it already. If so, it could be costing you a pretty penny. Let me explain why.

How many times have you said to yourself, "What would I do if I were the seller?" or, "If I were the seller, I wouldn't accept an offer like this, I'd be insulted." With these statements in mind you proceed to revamp your offer to one that seems more likely to be accepted! Why not let the seller decide what he will take and what he won't. Even if he doesn't like your offer his counter will be based on settling somewhere between his numbers and yours, so keep your numbers low.

Another typical example of self-negotiation is making offer after offer without receiving a counter-offer in writing from the seller.

Before I knew better, I offered $49,000 with $5,000 down on a triplex and tried to get ten years on a carryback at 10 percent interest. My first mistake was to call the seller's agent who had the property listed. Being a novice part-time realtor, he wrote a contract for me and promised to be in touch with me the next day.

The following evening, bubbling with enthusiasm, he told me the seller would go for it if I would raise the down payment to $8,000. I thought I had it made. All I had to give up was $3,000 more in cash. The agent handed me a new offer which I gladly signed, expecting to have an accepted contract within hours.

Back came the agent again showing great enthusiasm. If I would raise the interest rate to 12 percent he could get a signed contract, if only I would write one more offer. This time he returned with a request for a sales price of $55,000. It finally hit me that the seller was toying with me the entire time, never committing himself to a starting position. Before two people can negotiate, they must have starting points. In this situation, the seller kept getting the buyer's starting point higher and higher before he would actually begin. I realized I was negotiating with myself and stopped. We never did get together on a sale.

Such confusion is generally caused by an inexperienced real estate agent who returns from presenting your offer to the seller with a verbal commitment and expects you to write another offer. He has not obtained the seller's signature on a counter-offer and is taking the seller at his word. What generally happens is that you make a new offer, thinking it will be accepted, and are unpleasantly surprised to discover that a new verbal counter-offer is the only available option. You go back with a third, fourth, and fifth offer. The seller is testing you to see how far he can move ahead before the actual negotiations start. When you finally come to a halt and insist upon a signed, written counter-offer from the seller, negotiations will begin from your last written offer, not your first.

With this in mind NEVER write a second offer until you

have a signed counter-offer showing the intent of the seller. Now you can apply your knowledge and skill as a negotiator to get the right deal.

8. *He who cares the least wins.* Although the clauses in a contract are essential to negotiations, your mental attitude plays a key role in determining whether you will succeed or fail in the deal.

When negotiating ANY DEAL keep in mind the premise that, "He who cares the least wins." This is a very important concept and it is too often ignored. Too many times I have seen people buy property with the full knowledge that they are purchasing an alligator, paying more for the property than it is worth or paying a rate of interest that is higher than it should be.

Why do they do it? The most common reason is they can't walk away from the deal. They have put too much blood and sweat into making the deal work and they refuse to give it up. In any business deal it is essential that you remain objective and be prepared to forget the deal if it is not a good investment. You must be able to walk away and say, "I don't care. If I can't have it at my final price and terms I'll go on to another property." Who do you say it to? Yourself! You don't have to say it out loud. No one has to hear you. It is an attitude, a way of thinking that enables you to negotiate toward achieving your goals, and realize when your goals cannot be reached.

Don't trap yourself into not being able to care the least. Beware of these roadblocks:

1. Don't spend the money before you close the deal. By committing the funds or planning where the money will go, you are weakening your ability to walk away.

2. Don't tell anyone about the great deal you are putting together. Your ego and your pride may force you to purchase

something you wouldn't have if you hadn't told everyone about it!

3. Don't let brokers, agents, or peers persuade you to buy property that you know is not a good investment. Think and decide for yourself—and again, walk away if necessary.

9. *Eleventh-hour negotiations.* Eleventh-hour negotiations occur many times in real estate transactions. They often take place just before a critical point in the bargaining, usually at closing. This signifies to you that a crisis is near and that if the two sides can't come to an agreement soon, there will be a problem. When two people have a close of escrow coming up, one of them is usually vulnerable—the one who needs the deal the most. Nine times out of ten this will be the seller. From the day the seller accepted the contract, he has already mentally spent the money he'll receive. Satisfied that the money is coming, he generally makes plans based on the closing. Should the deal not close, he could face a severe cash problem. This of course puts the buyer into the driver's seat. As long as the buyer doesn't ask for too much, he can get concessions. Concessions that could be the frosting on the cake.

For example, what do you think the seller will do if you refuse to close escrow until he agrees to pay the escrow fee? Or better yet, do you think the seller will kill the deal if you, the buyer, confess one day before closing that you are short on cash and the seller will have to take $1,000 or $2,000 less cash at closing?

His first reaction will be one of anger and he may refuse to close, calling you every name in the book. But the bottom line is that once he thinks it over he will probably give in, in order to make the deal.

In eleventh-hour negotiations you must picture yourself in a poker game. It's now up to the seller to decide whether you are bluffing or are willing to go through with your threat not to close. Is he going to risk the entire deal on the possibility that you are telling the truth? Or, will he bend a little to make the deal work? This is the exciting part of negotiations.

What if he "calls your hand?" Will you walk away or back off and return to the original terms of the contract? You must be prepared with a game plan. If you do insist on holding your ground, you must be willing to walk away from the deal. If he backs off after a bluff and agrees to close, then be ready to close. The possibilities are unlimited and the answers become more apparent as you improve your skills.

10. *One-last-shot method of negotiation.* There will be times when a deal will not gel regardless of how good you are at negotiating. The seller will hold his ground and if you have followed your guidelines of sound investments, you will hold yours. The two positions do not, and cannot, come together. When this happens there is still one more shot to take.

It will only be successful if used when all else has failed, and once it is used, your options to try other methods have ended. It is not a method that will work very often. As a matter of fact, it will fail more often than not, and it should only be used when all else has failed.

In desperation at the end of the negotiation session, stand up, walk toward the door looking depressed, turn back to the seller and say, "I am really sorry we couldn't come to terms. I must be doing something wrong, because I really want to buy your building. I know you want to sell it and I know you feel you are selling it at a fair price, but it doesn't make financial sense to me at your price (terms, etc.). Is there something that I am missing or don't understand?" The next few seconds are very vital! Act sincere. You must look dejected. You are appealing to an emotional instinct in most people—that need to help others. If you truly look like you need help, you will see a change in the opposition. Instead of looking at you as an enemy, the seller will now become your friend and will actually help you buy his property. If all goes right you will end up with the concessions you need.

Remember, this does not work often. But when it does, it is very gratifying, because you have utilized a skill that only a few people can master.

If it works, you have a deal that would have passed you by. If not, you have lost nothing.

Recently, I used this last-ditch effort on the purchase of a triplex. The seller and I couldn't agree on either price or terms and we were at a stalemate. I stood up and hit the seller with this final shot. It must have hit home, because he never let me reach the door. With practically no break in the conversation, he motioned me back to my chair and said, "You know, I probably wouldn't buy this triplex under the terms I've set. Let's see if we can work out something more reasonable. I guess I can take a little less cash and a lower price. I'll still make a good profit." I had him negotiating for me and I didn't have to do a thing. Before he finished, he had taken out his calculator and spent five minutes punching numbers. Finishing, he turned to me, adding, "Here is the best I can do and still live with it." His offer was for less than I had originally intended. He did a better job for me than I could have done.

Associate With High Producers

This is a concept most ambitious investors learn early in their careers. Observe the leaders in your city or community. Whom do you see them with at seminars, meetings, and social functions? Almost invariably it will be with people like themselves, or even more successful investors who have influence and are admired throughout the community for their accomplishments.

These people are engaged in what I call "success through osmosis." They are keenly aware of whom they are seen with because they know that if they are consistently observed with "winners," others will conclude that they must be good performers too. They also realize that association with individuals who are considered leaders in the world is not always to their benefit.

This behavior may not sit well with you, but remember, it is an integral part of what you are trying to learn—the negotiation game. If you need to justify such actions to yourself before you can behave this way, simply acknowledge that we all can learn much more through association with successful people than with other people who never take risks.

Increase Your Influence in Negotiations

We discussed influence in an earlier chapter as the ability to motivate others into your way of thinking—without their knowing it. In your negotiations, the ability to influence others will go hand in hand with winning the game of give and take. Influence is largely a function of status and exposure in society —both of which can be developed if you put your mind to it. Here are a few tips to increase your ability to influence others.

Develop professional relationships with investors who are recognized as having authority and success. Your association with these individuals will add credibility to your own endeavors. You will demonstrate more with behavior than with words. Associating with and acting like a person with influence and power will lead others to believe you are a person who gets things done.

Becoming informed about situations around you and educating yourself in all your endeavors enables you to influence people with your knowledge. In your transactions you will often be called upon to state facts and know proper procedures. Keeping informed of the economic, social, and political aspects of real estate will allow you to exert your influence with confidence.

In any negotiation, how you influence the other person will also depend largely on your ability to present relevant information in a tactful manner. Tact is a very important consideration. It is a respect for the efforts and responsibility of the other person. Even the most aggressive negotiators know when it is appropriate to use tact in their negotiations. My favorite story about tact is one told by one of the greatest storytellers of all time, John Steinbeck:

> Two men were meeting in a bar when the subject of Green Bay, Wisconsin, came up. The first man said, "Green Bay is a real nice place." The second responded, "What's so nice about it? The only things ever to come out of Green Bay were the Packers and ugly whores."
> "Now you wait just one minute, buddy," said the first man. "My wife is from Green Bay."
> "Oh," replied the second man. "She is? What position does she play?"

On Winning and Losing Negotiations

If you lose a tennis match, what have you really lost? Nothing, really. You may have hit the ball as hard as the other guy, but your shots didn't make it over the net or land within bounds. It is amazing how preoccupied some negotiators can become with the concept of winning, often to the detriment of the game.

If you need to win in order to prove yourself, you've lost all the chances of being an effective negotiator. If the game becomes bigger than life and you find yourself obsessed, enraged, depressed, or whatever, you need to reassess the situation and the philosophy of quality negotiations. You see, winning the game of give and take requires an attitude that places less emphasis on winning and more emphasis on getting a good deal. Ironically, the less emphasis you place on winning, the more likely you are to come out ahead.

Become Your Own Expert Negotiator

Ultimately, after you have read enough books, attended a few seminars, and negotiated a lot of deals, you will become an expert negotiator. As you incorporate the information of other experts, your own style will be more clear.

What is the best way to become an expert negotiator? Practice. After reading this book, go out and write a few contracts, use the weasel clauses, exercise the techniques I've spelled out for you. Use your *chutzpah* to create situations that make deals work. Then go over your mistakes, look for areas where you may have felt vulnerable, and correct those areas.

How did the seller react when you insisted on a carryback for fifteen years at 7 percent interest? How did you respond? Did you act or react? Did you give in or trade off? What did it feel like when a seller gave you a "final offer," one which you absolutely couldn't accept. Did you want to give in? Or stand firm? Did you have thoughts like, "This is the best deal, the only deal, don't let it slip through your fingers now. There won't be another like it." If so, then I suggest you review the earlier chapters until you achieve the "he who cares the least, wins" attitude.

Learn from your mistakes. Negotiating real estate is an art that comes with practice and experience. Then, go out and teach others how to negotiate their real estate deals. There is no better way to learn about a subject than to teach someone else how to do it.

Develop Your Ability—Then Use It

There is a good measure of self-knowledge required to be an effective negotiator. It has been speculated that many investors, without knowing it, go into deals secretly wanting to lose. Some skim the classified ad sections eliminating those properties that "aren't good deals" until no ads are left. They jump in with high hopes, but feeling vaguely guilty. Guilty over "risking" the family savings or trying to "get something for nothing." They get caught up in "analysis paralysis," and never negotiate a complete deal, or they sell their properties at a loss.

In any event, whether or not you intend to, many people do lose. If this book can save you a few dollars on the next house you purchase (negotiating rock-bottom price and terms), or on taxes (especially through the ACRS tax law passed by President Reagan in 1981 which gives investors a much greater depreciation each year), or on your next building, then I will be happy. But, if you take the knowledge you gain from these pages, apply the techniques, and USE YOUR *CHUTZPAH* to negotiate the purchase, or sale, of a building that makes you thousands of dollars, then I will be delighted, and proud to invite you into the realm of winners and leaders. Welcome to the 1 percent.

| Items for Negotiation

Each contract has many different points that need to be negotiated. Too often you take many of these for granted and accept the contract as being "standard."

Here are the major items to be negotiated from the viewpoint of both the buyer and the seller.

1. Purchase Price

BUYER: Set your goals and then offer at least 10 percent below your goal. Remember, your goals must be at "wholesale" or "sub-wholesale" prices so you can get out if you have to.

SELLER: After you have figured out what the property is worth and what you will accept (hopefully the same price), your asking should be set at least 10 percent higher than the required amount.

2. Earnest Deposit

BUYER: Wants to delay deposit as long as possible and writes on the contract, after the name of the company receiving the deposit: "To be deposited upon removal of contingencies."

Never give the money to the seller. Either give it to a title company, a real estate company, or an attorney. Since you will have five weeks to remove contingencies (see No. 10) you are tying down the property for a long period with no money down.

SELLER: Many sellers want an earnest deposit and therefore should delete any clause similar in nature to the buyer's choice above and should counter with: "Earnest deposit to be deposited upon acceptance of this agreement."

This is one of the items I "lose" in order to win a more important one later. If the seller has a contingency clause in the contract and can get his deposit back, I don't see a need to open an escrow account or have an attorney do all the paperwork until the contingencies have been removed and we have a firm contract.

3. Down Payment

BUYER: Offer either no down payment or as little as possible (to cover closing costs, etc.). Your object is to gain maximum leverage.

SELLER: Ask for "cash to mortgage" to get all your money out. Don't be fooled by all of the purchaser's great reasons for you to take little or nothing down.

4. Debt Service

BUYER: Wants to assume existing mortgages and have seller take a carryback for the difference at a low interest rate for at least seven years. Beware of "due-on-sale" or "acceleration" clause.

SELLER: Wants a wraparound for the entire amount at the current interest rate so that he may make the difference between the low interest rate on the existing mortgages and the high rate on the wraparound. Seller wants a balloon payment in no more than three years.

5. Personal Property

BUYER: Wants a separate bill of sale with a definite price on all personal property to establish a depreciation schedule for the faster depreciation allowed for personal property.

SELLER: Wants to sell the land and the building and give the personal property away since it has no value. Any money received for personal property above the remaining tax basis (which is usually zero within a few years of purchase) will be taxed at ordinary income tax rates.

6. Condition of Property

BUYER: Would like to have both the seller and the real estate agent or broker warrant the working condition of the property both at closing and for one year from closing. If seller doesn't agree, try to get seller to obtain an insurance policy on the life-support systems in the building for one year.

SELLER: Ideal situation is to sell it in "as is" condition. Make sure contract states, "Purchaser has inspected the property and after making said inspection agrees to accept property in 'as is' condition."

7. Additional Payments

BUYER: After stating monthly payment amount, add the words "or more." This allows the purchaser to pay as he wants each month and each year toward the principal and can pay off the loan anytime he wishes to do so. This prevents prepayment penalties and lock-in mortgages.

SELLER: Wants a prepayment penalty in case of early payoff, or wants a lock-in clause preventing early payoff or some combination of the two. Try not to allow extra principal payments toward the end of the calendar year when you will have to pay taxes on the money received the following April.

8. Remedies for Not Completing Purchase and Sale

BUYER: If buyer wants out, then the forfeit of the earnest deposit is the only penalty. If the seller wants out, the buyer wants the right to make the seller go through with the contract (specific performance).

SELLER: If seller wants out, the returning of the earnest deposit should allow him to get out of the contract. If the buyer wants out, seller wants the right to make buyer go through with the transaction (specific performance).

9. Purchaser to Have Right to Accompany Agent Upon Presentation

BUYER: This gives the buyer the right to meet with the seller if negotiations bog down. Let the agent act for you until a snag in the negotiations arises.

SELLER: This clause does not affect you, so there should be no objection to it.

10. Contingency Clause (All-Inclusive Weasel Clause)

BUYER: Naturally, you want time to get out of any contract if your inspections show differences from the seller's original information. This clause can also be used to get out of any contract for any reason whatsoever. (Thereby the name "all-inclusive weasel clause".)

"This offer contingent upon inspection and approval of all books, records, leases, personal management contracts, preliminary title reports, underlying encumbrances and physical inspection of the property."

"Purchaser to have fourteen working days from receipt of the above to remove all contingencies in writing or this offer is null and void and all earnest money to be returned in full."

SELLER: Would prefer to have no contingencies. However if he receives a "weasel clause," he can counter with his "anti-weasel clause," which will allow the buyer to tie up the property only for as long as the seller permits.

". . . However, should the seller receive a bona fide offer, he may, at his option, give purchaser forty-eight hours to remove all contingencies in writing, or this offer is null and void and all earnest money to be returned in full."

11. Contingency Removal

BUYER: Wants contract to die and earnest money to be returned unless contingencies are removed in writing.

SELLER: Wants contingencies automatically removed unless there is written notice to the contrary.

12. Transferring Title

BUYER: Wants seller to pay for title policy and all closing costs and in some states would prefer to give abstract of title instead of title policy.

SELLER: Wants buyer to pay for title policy and all closing costs and in some states would prefer to give abstract of title instead of title policy.

13. Deposits

BUYER: Wants both refundable and nonrefundable deposits credited to him at closing since he will have to clean the apartment after a current tenant moves out.

SELLER: Wants to give credit for refundable deposits only, since nonrefundable deposits were spent cleaning apartments when a tenant moved in.

14. Rents, Taxes, and Insurance

BUYER: Wants all of the above to be prorated as of the day of closing.

SELLER: Wants no proration of any kind.

15. Late Payments

BUYER: Wants no late-payment clauses in the contract except those in the encumbrances being assumed.

SELLER: Wants to have late-payment penalty put into any carryback or wraparound agreement written for the new contract. This is the clause most often left out by the seller through forgetfulness.

16. Subordination

BUYER: Must make sure the seller will agree to subordinate his carryback to any refinancing needed to cover short-term notes.

"Seller agrees that his carryback shall be inferior and subordinate to any existing loans and to any replacement, renewal, or extension thereof."

This allows you to extend any short-term financing without pushing the new note into a costly junior position.

SELLER: Never wants to allow any subordination clause into the contract because it will weaken your position and your security.

17. Type of Sale

There are many ways to take title. The following applies to most states, although you should check the rules and regulations at the local level.

BUYER: Wants to purchase in the following order: a. Mortgage: Purchaser receives title and gives a mortgage to the lender. This takes the longest period of time for the seller to regain possession in the case of default. It could take as long as eighteen months in some states. b. Trust deed: Purchaser receives title and gives a trust deed to a third party which shall be activated in case of default. In most states it takes the seller 90 to 120 days to regain possession and title to the property. c. Land contract (agreement of sale, contract for deed): Title does not pass to purchaser until all terms of the contract have been satisfied. Since seller retains title, he can regain possession in as little as thirty days in some states.

SELLER: Prefers reverse order, however, both parties should investigate all the pros and cons of each type of ownership.

18. Permission to Show Property During Contingency Period

BUYER: To make sure you don't end up with an "alligator" when you buy a single-family home as an income property, you will need time and access to the property to make sure you can secure a tenant at the correct rental rate.

"Purchaser to have right to show property to prospective tenants during contingency period."

SELLER: If it helps the deal, go along with it. Not every term of every contract is going to be good for one party and bad for the other. Some clauses are good for both parties.

| Recommendations for Further Education

BOOKS AND CASSETTE TAPES

How to Become Financially Independent by Investing in Real Estate, Albert J. Lowry, Ph.D. Three years on the *New York Times* Best Seller List, this revised edition is the basic primer on the subject of real estate and the book that got me started.

$17.95.

How to Manage Real Estate Successfully in Your Spare Time, Albert J. Lowry, Ph.D. A unique, comprehensive guide to owning and managing residential real estate. This is the bible on being a landlord. You can't have tenants without this as your reference book.

$29.95

Hidden Fortunes, Albert J. Lowry, Ph.D. New tactics for a new era in real estate investment. Learn where to find the real estate bargains. This best-seller will take you through the "hidden fortunes of the Eighties."

$16.95

101 Purchase Offers Sellers Can't Resist, Dave Del Dotto. An innovative, creative approach to finding common denominators to make a deal. A book I call "a great crutch" for those who need help writing contracts.

$49.00

Control Without Ownership (workbook and six cassette tapes), Phil Drummond. Phil makes this technique look simple with this package.

$125.00

Negotiating—Winning the Game of Give and Take, Tony Hoffman. If you like learning by tape, my six-cassette tape package with workbook

249

is a full, one-day negotiation workshop. Comes with a bonus tape on negotiating foreclosure properties.

$145.00

Paper (workbook and eight tapes), Joe Land. The name is simple, and Joe takes difficult ideas and makes them simple with easy-to-follow illustrations on how to use paper and mortgages to buy property.

$165.00

Tax Strategies (workbook and eight tapes), Joe Land. The best real estate tax course I have listened to. It has saved me thousands of dollars.

$165.00

Cash Flow, Cash Flow, Cash Flow (workbook and six tapes), Mike and Irene Milin. And they mean it with their ideas. They share how they bought 134 houses in three years.

$129.00

Foreclosure Systems (workbook and eight tapes), Hal Morris. Hal's seminar on foreclosures saved me $160,000 in one deal. Need I say more? If you want to learn the foreclosure market, this is the product for you.

$225.00

How to Stop Foreclosures, Hal Morris. Required reading for anyone in trouble today.

$14.95

Concepts and Mechanics of Exchanges (workbook and six tapes), Danny Santucci. This cassette series by Danny, attorney and realtor, is the most complete in the business!

$175.00

How to Win With Equity Sharing (workbook and six tapes), Barney Zick. The king of equity sharing, Barney Zick, shows you step by step how to do it. The method of the Eighties, this is Barney at his best.

$195.00

NEWSLETTERS

Impact Reports and Update Newsletter. "Written by experts, *Impact Reports* are packed with hard-hitting information to use in your investment strategy," says Al Lowry. These are how-to mini-books, plus an eight-page newsletter. When you subscribe you get ten future *Impact Reports* plus ten timely *Update Newsletters.*

$97.00 for one year

Joe Land's Tax Tips. One of the most comprehensive newsletters on taxes for anyone who wants to keep up on all the changes in real estate tax laws.

$48.00 for one year

APPENDIX C: My Standard Residential Earnest Money Contract

STANDARD RESIDENTIAL EARNEST MONEY CONTRACT

1. PARTIES: _____ (Seller) agrees
   to sell and convey to _____ (Buyer)
   County, (State), known as _____ (Address).

2. PROPERTY: Lot _____ Addition, City of _____, Block _____, or as described on attached exhibit,
   together with the following fixtures, if any: curtain rods, drapery rods, venetian blinds, window shades, screens and shutters,
   awnings, wall-to-wall carpeting, mirrors fixed in place, attic fans, permanently installed heating and air conditioning units
   and equipment, lighting and plumbing fixtures, TV antennas, mail boxes, water softeners, shrubbery and all other property
   owned by Seller and attached to the above described real property. All property sold by this contract is called "Property".

3. CONTRACT SALES PRICE:
   A. The ☐ Exact ☐ Approximate   Cash down payment payable at closing .... $ _____
   B. Buyer's assumption of the unpaid balance of promissory note (the Note) payable in present
      monthly installments of $ _____, including principal and interest and any reserve
      deposits, with Buyer's first installments payable to _____ on _____, 19 ____, the
      assumed principal balance of which at closing (allowing for an agreed $250 variance) will
      be .... $ _____
   C. Any balance of Sales Price to be evidenced by a second lien note payable to (check #1 or #2 below):
      ☐ 1. Seller, bearing interest at the rate of _____ % per annum, in
         ☐ lump sum on or before _____, _____ or more per
         ☐ principal and interest installments of $ _____
            _____, with first installment payable on _____
      ☐ 2. Third Party in principal and interest installments not in excess of $ _____
         per month and in the ☐ Exact ☐ Approximate (check "Approximate" only if A above
         and D below are "Exact") amount of .... $ _____
   D. The ☐ Exact ☐ Approximate total Sales Price of (Sum of A, B and C above) .... $ _____

4. FINANCING CONDITIONS: If a noteholder on assumption (i) requires buyer to pay an assumption fee in excess of
   $ _____ and seller declines to pay such excess (ii) raises the existing interest rate above _____ % or (iii)
   requires approval of buyer or can accelerate the Note and Buyer does not receive from the Noteholder written approval and
   acceleration waiver prior to the Closing Date, Buyer may terminate this contract and the Earnest Money shall be refunded.
   Buyer shall apply for the approval and waiver under (iii) above within 7 days from the effective date hereof and shall make
   every effort to obtain the same.

5. EARNEST MONEY: $ _____ is herewith tendered and is to be deposited as Earnest Money with
   _____ as Escrow Agent

... Seller at Seller's expense shall furnish an Owner's Policy of Title Insurance (the Title Policy) issued by _____ in amount of Sales Price at or after Closing.

7. PROPERTY CONDITION (Check "A" or "B")

   ☐ A. Buyer accepts the Property in its present condition, subject only to _____

   ☐ B. Buyer requires inspections and repairs required by the Property Condition Addendum (the Addendum).

   Upon Seller's receipt of all loan approvals and inspection reports Seller shall commence and complete prior to closing all required repairs at Seller's expense.

   All inspections, reports and repairs required of Seller by this contract and the addendum shall not exceed $_____. If Seller fails to complete such requirements, Buyer may do so and Seller shall be liable up to the amount specified and the same paid from the proceeds of the sale. If such expenditures exceed the stated amount and Seller refuses to pay such excess, Buyer may pay the additional cost or accept the Property with the limited repairs and this sale shall be closed as scheduled, or Buyer may terminate this contract and the Earnest Money shall be refunded to Buyer, Broker and sales associates have no responsibility or liability for repair or replacement of any of the Property.

8. CONTINGENCIES: This offer contingent upon inspection and approval of all books, records, leases, personal management contracts, underlying encumbrances, preliminary title report, and physical inspection of the building. Buyer to have fourteen working days from receipt of the above to remove all contingencies in writing or this offer is null and void and all Earnest Money to be returned in full.

9. SUBORDINATION: Should this contract call for the Seller to carry back his equity in the form of note secured by the property being purchased, the Seller agrees to subordinate said note to any replacement, renewal, or extension of any senior encumbrance on said property.

10. ACCOMPANIMENT: Buyer to have right to accompany agent upon presentation of contract.

11. RIGHT TO SHOW: Buyer to have right to show property to prospective tenants during contingency period.

12. 1031 EXCHANGE: Both Buyer and Seller agree to participate in a 1031 Tax-deferred exchange at the cost and risk of the party benefiting by the exchange.

13. BROKER'S FEE: _____ Listing Broker (_____ %) and _____ Co-Broker (_____ %), as Real Estate Broker (the Broker). has negotiated this, sale and Seller agrees to pay Broker in _____ County, _____, on consummation of this sale or on Seller's default (unless otherwise provided herein) a total cash fee of _____ of the total Sale Price, which Escrow Agent may pay from the sale proceeds.

14. CLOSING: The closing of the sale (the Closing Date) shall be on or before _____, 19 _____ or within 7 days after objections to title have been cured, whichever date is later.

15. POSSESSION: The possession of the property shall be delivered to Buyer on _____ in its present or required improved condition, ordinary wear and tear except. Any possession by Buyer prior to or by Seller after Closing Date shall establish a landlord-tenant at sufferance relationship between the parties.

16. SPECIAL PROVISIONS: See addendum for special provisions.

17. PRORATION: Taxes, insurance, rents, interest and maintenance fees, if any □ SHALL □ SHALL NOT be prorated to the Closing Date. If these are not prorated, all funds held in reserve for payment of taxes, maintenance fees and insurance and the insurance policy shall be transferred to the Buyer by the Seller without cost to Buyer.

18. SALES EXPENSE TO BE PAID IN CASH AT OUR PRIOR TO CLOSING: Preparing Deed, preparing and recording Deed of Trust to Secure Assumption, all inspections, reports and repairs required of Seller herein and in the Addendum and 1/2 of escrow fee shall be Seller's expense. All other costs and expenses incurred in connection with this contract which are not recited herein to be the obligation of Seller, shall be the obligation of Buyer. Unless otherwise paid, before Buyer shall be entitled to refund of Earnest Money, any such costs and expenses shall be deducted therefrom and paid to the creditors entitled thereto. If any sales expenses exceed the maximum amount herein stipulated to be paid by either party, either party may terminate this contract unless the other party agrees to pay such excess.

19. TITLE APPROVAL: If Title Policy is furnished, the Title Policy shall guarantee Buyer's Title to be good and indefeasible subject only to (i) restrictive covenants affecting the Property (ii) any discrepancies, conflicts or shortages in area or boundary lines of any encroachments, or any overlapping of improvements (iii) all taxes of the current and subsequent years (iv) any existing building and zoning ordinances (v) rights of parties in possession (vi) any liens assumed or created as security for the sale consideration and (vii) any reservations or exceptions contained in the Deed. If title objections are disclosed, Seller shall have 30 days to cure the same. Exceptions permitted in the Deed and zoning ordinances shall not be valid objections to title. Seller shall furnish at Seller's expense tax statements showing no delinquent taxes and a General Warranty Deed conveying title subjects only to liens securing debt created or assumed as part of the consideration, taxes for the current year, usual restrictive covenants and utility easements common to the platted sub-division of which the Property is a part and any other reservations or exceptions acceptable to Buyer. Each note herein provided shall be secured by Vendor's and Deed of Trust liens. A vendor's lien shall be retained and a Deed of Trust to Secure Assumption required, which shall be automatically released on execution and delivery of a release by noteholder. In case of dispute as to the form of Deed, Note(s) or Deed(s) of Trust, such shall be upon a form prepared by the State of, _____

20. CASUALTY LOSS: If any part of Property is damaged or destroyed by fire or other casualty loss, Seller shall restore the same to its previous condition as soon as reasonably possible, but in any event by Closing Date; and if Seller is unable to do so without fault, this contract shall terminate and Earnest Money shall be refunded with no Broker fee due

21. DEFAULT: If Buyer fails to comply herewith, Seller may terminate this contract and receive the Earnest Money as liquidated damages, one-half of which (but not exceeding the herein recited Broker's fee) shall be paid by Seller to Broker in full payment for Broker's services. If Seller is unable without fault to deliver Abstract or Title Policy or to make any non-casualty repairs required herein within the time herein specified, Buyer may either terminate this contract and receive the Earnest Money as the sole remedy, and no Broker's fee shall be earned, or extend the time up to 30 days. If Seller fails to comply herewith for any other reason, Buyer may (i) terminate this contract and receive the Earnest Money, thereby releasing Seller from this contract (ii) enforce specified performance hereof or (iii) seek such other relief as may be provided by law.

22. ATTORNEY'S FEES: Any signatory to this contract who is the prevailing party in any legal proceeding against any other signatory brought under or with relation to this contract or transaction shall be additionally entitled to recover court costs and reasonable attorney fees from the non-prevailing party.

23. ESCROW: Earnest Money is deposited with Escrow Agent with the understanding that Escrow Agent (i) does not assume or have any liability for performance of non-performance of any party (ii) has the right to require the receipt, release and authorization in writing of all parties before paying the deposit to any party and (iii) is not liable for interest or other charge on the funds held. If any party unreasonably fails to agree in writing to an appropriate release of Earnest Money, then such party shall be liable to the other parties to the extent provided in paragraph 22. At closing Earnest Money shall be applied to any cash down payment required, next to Buyer's closing costs and any excess refunded to Buyer. Before Buyer shall be entitled to refund of Earnest Money, any actual expenses incurred or paid on Buyer's behalf shall be deducted therefrom and paid to the creditors entitled thereto.

24. REPRESENTATIONS: Seller represents that unless securing payment of the Note there will be no Title I liens, unrecorded liens or Uniform Commercial Code liens against any of the Property on Closing Date, that loan(s) will be without default, and reserve deposits will not be deficient. If any representation above is untrue this contract may be terminated by Buyer and the Earnest Money shall be refunded without delay. Representations shall survive closing.

25. AGREEMENT OF PARTIES: This contract contains the entire agreement of both parties and cannot be changed except by their written consent.

26. CONSULT YOUR ATTORNEY: This is intended to be a legally binding contract. READ IT CAREFULLY. If you do not understand the effect of any part, consult your attorney BEFORE signing.

EXECUTED IN MULTIPLE ORIGINALS effective the _____ day of _____ , 19 _____ .

_____   _____
Buyer   Buyer

Accepted in multiple originals effective the _____ day of _____ , 19 _____ .

_____   _____
Seller   Seller

Index

259